W9-AMK-883

Webster University
A Century of Defining Moments

Webster
UNIVERSITY

Press

Copyright © 2015, Webster University
All rights reserved.

Published in cooperation with
Reedy Press
www.reedypress.com

No part of this publication may be reproduced or transmitted in any form
or by any means, electronic or mechanical, including photocopy, recording,
or any information storage and retrieval system, without permission in
writing from the publisher.

Permissions may be sought directly from Webster University at the following
mailing address or via our website at www.webster.edu/wup:

Webster University Press
c/o Webster University Library
470 East Lockwood Avenue
Saint Louis, Missouri 63119-3194

Library of Congress Control Number: 2015945795
ISBN: 9780982161500

Printed in the United States of America
15 16 17 18 19   5 4 3 2 1

TABLE OF CONTENTS

Acknowledgments · V

Board of Trustees, 2014-15 · VI

Introductions by President Elizabeth (Beth) J. Stroble and Provost Julian Z. Schuster · X

Foreword by Chairman Steven O. Swyers · XII

Preface by Centennial Planning Chair Elizabeth Robb · XIII

From Local College to Worldwide University · 1

The Courage to Act Produces a Singular College · 3

A Tradition of Inclusive Leadership · 10

The Home Campus Evolves · 23

Reaching out to Working Adults · 34

Support for Active Military and Veterans · 42

Broadening Perspectives through Global Opportunities · 50

A Distinctive Approach to the Educational Experience · 77

Cultivating Excellence in Teaching, Learning, and Scholarship · 78

Unconventional Paths to Quality Learning Experiences · 90

Student-Centered Learning in the Disciplines · 102

Growing School Spirit · 204

Enriching Learning through Community Partnerships · 218

An Enduring Spirit of Caring and Inclusiveness · 227

Support for Webster's Mission · 228

A Commitment to a Diverse and Inclusive University · 238

Social Justice and Community Service · 250

Environmental Sustainability Yesterday and Today for the Webster of Tomorrow · 262

The Future · 269

The Centennial Year: Bridge to the Future · 270

A Visionary Plan for the Future · 275

Endnotes · 286

Photo and Public Art Credits · 290

WEBSTER UNIVERSITY

1915 **W** 2015

Global Impact for
THE NEXT CENTURY

ACKNOWLEDGMENTS

Many individuals dedicated their time and expertise to make this book a reality.

Thank you to:

President Elizabeth (Beth) J. Stroble and Provost Julian Z. Schuster

Board of Trustees Chair Steven O. Swyers

Centennial Planning Chair Elizabeth Robb

Writers Patricia Corrigan and Dave Lange

Editors Eileen Condon, Kathy Gaynor, and Laura Rein

Webster's Global Marketing Communications team for writing, photography, and videography assistance

Reedy Press President Josh Stevens

Design Team Barbara Northcott and Julie Sturma of Reedy Press

And a special thank you to Professor Joe Schuster, Betsy Rogers, Debra Schwartz, Professor Fred Stopsky, and all who worked on Webster's history project, and to Sr. Mary Mangan, whose history of the first fifty years of Webster University was an invaluable resource and inspiration to us all.

2014–15 WEBSTER UNIVERSITY BOARD OF TRUSTEES

Steven O. Swyers, Chair of the Board
Partner, Ret.
PricewaterhouseCoopers, LLP

Amelia J. Bond, Vice Chair of the Board
President and Chief Executive Officer
Greater Saint Louis Community
Foundation

Elizabeth (Beth) J. Stroble
President
Webster University

Julian Schuster
Provost, Sr. Vice President and
Chief Operating Officer
Webster University

Greg Gunderson
Treasurer
Vice President and Chief Financial Officer
Webster University

Jeanelle Wiley
University Secretary
Webster University

Sheila Baxter
Brigadier General, Ret.
Western Regional Medical Command

James (Lynn) Britton
President and CEO
Mercy Health System

Dale Cammon
Chairman and Co-Chief Executive
Bryant Group, Inc.

Robert M. Cox, Jr.
Sr. Vice President in Administration, Ret.
Emerson Electric Co.

Clark S. Davis
Consultant
HOK Group, Inc.

Michael DeHaven
Sr. VP and General Counsel
BJC HealthCare

Alison N. Ferring
Civic Leader

Webster University | A Century of Defining Moments

VI

Steven L. Finerty
Chairman
Argent Capital Management

Marilyn Fox
Civic Leader

John (Jack) Galmiche III
President and CEO
Nine Network of Public Media

Edward L. Glotzbach
Vice Chairman
Information Services Group, Inc.

Tracy E. Hart
President
Tarlton Corporation

Laura Herring
Founder and Chairwoman
The Impact Group

Peter Wyse Jackson
President
Missouri Botanical Garden

Carmen Jacob
President
NextGen Information Services, Inc.

Kristin M. Johnson
Principal
Edward Jones

Christopher McGee
Curriculum Coordinator for
Science & Social Studies K-8
Webster Groves School District

Lee J. Metcalf
Rear Admiral, Ret.
United States Navy

Michael Neidorff
Chairman and CEO
Centene Corporation

Gregory L. Nelson
Sr. Vice President, Gen. Counsel,
and Secretary
Ameren Corporation

WEBSTER UNIVERSITY BOARD OF TRUSTEES

Webster University | A Century of Defining Moments

Brenda Newberry
Partner, Nesher LLC
Founder and Chair, Ret.
The Newberry Group, Inc.

Jane Robert
President
Renaissance Francaise-USA

John A. (Jack) Schreiber
President and COO
Commerce Bank of St. Louis

William W. Snyder
Executive VP and CFO
Enterprise Holdings, Inc.

David Steward
Chairman
World Wide Technology, Inc.

Anthony (Tony) Thompson
Chairman & CEO
Kwame Building Group, Inc.

Eugene (Gene) Toombs
Chairman Emeritus
MiTek Industries, Inc.

Markus Trice
Co-founder and Managing Partner
Compass Equity Advisors

James D. Weddle
Managing Partner
Edward Jones

Patricia D. Whitaker
CEO
Arcturis

Lynn Wittels
President and CEO
St. Louis Jewish Community Center

Scott E. Wuesthoff
Brigadier General, USAF Ret.
Director, Domestic and International
F-15 Programs
The Boeing Company

Douglas H. Yaeger
Chairman, President and CEO, Ret.
The Laclede Group Inc.

Michael Zambrana
Owner, President, CEO
Pangea Group

LIFE TRUSTEE
Ambassador George H. Walker III
Chairman Emeritus
Stifel, Nicolaus & Co., Inc.

EMERITA MEMBER
Jane B. Hart

HONORARY TRUSTEES
Robert Q. Costas
Franklin A. Jacobs

INTRODUCTION

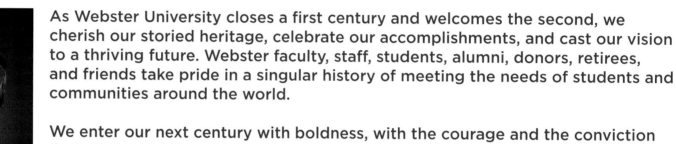

As Webster University closes a first century and welcomes the second, we cherish our storied heritage, celebrate our accomplishments, and cast our vision to a thriving future. Webster faculty, staff, students, alumni, donors, retirees, and friends take pride in a singular history of meeting the needs of students and communities around the world.

We enter our next century with boldness, with the courage and the conviction that what we do at Webster makes a difference. Just as we have transformed students for individual excellence and global citizenship, so have we been transformed.

Through our global commitments to innovation, inclusive leadership, student-centered experiences, academic and operational excellence, and strategic and sustainable development, we will assure Webster's global impact for the next century.

I am honored to serve as Webster University's eleventh president at this defining moment in our history. May our legacy together provide as much pride and joy for those who come after us as the stories captured in these pages do for us in this Centennial year.

In this book and throughout our Centennial celebration, we honor Webster's history and the dedication of all who have made Webster their home in our first century. This Centennial year is one to treasure as we together assure Webster's home in the world for the next century.

Elizabeth (Beth) J. Stroble
President

The publication of this book is one way to honor our long and distinguished history. In the past 100 years, Webster University has grown deep roots into communities around the world, and we take pride in documenting how our mission and values have profoundly impacted students, and through them, society.

Our history has given us a firm foundation on which to stand and face the future, because a second, and more important, way to honor Webster University's past is to create its future—our next 100 years. Standing on the solid bedrock of what has come before, we are purposefully and intentionally charting the future of this great institution. Webster today is imaginative, inquisitive, innovative, integrative—characteristics which will take us to new heights and new horizons in the years to come.

I am proud to be a part of this great university and honored to work with my colleagues and friends as we embark on new and exciting pathways.

Julian Z. Schuster
Provost, Senior Vice President and Chief Operating Officer

FOREWORD

In Webster University's Centennial year, first as a Board of Trustees member and now as Board of Trustees chair, I am reminded of my place in Webster University's history. From Mother Dolorine Powers, the first superior in 1916 to Sandy Zimmerman, the first lay board chair in 1967, to the many dedicated Board of Trustees members through the years, we are all connected. Our experiences are intertwined throughout the 100 years of Webster's history, connecting us not only with one another but with Webster's faculty, students, staff, and more than 176,000 alumni around the world.

As Webster University enters its second century serving students in communities around the world, I, along with other members of the Board of Trustees look forward to continuing our stewardship of this incredible institution so that Webster University maintains its proud place in history.

In 1915, Webster University was poised on a path for growth. In 2015, we find ourselves at that same doorstep, moving forward with swift and focused intent as we continue our commitment to preparing students for an ever-changing world.

Steven O. Swyers
Board of Trustees Chair

PREFACE

As a former Webster University student, former Board of Trustees member, entrepreneur and business owner, and long-term friend and supporter of Webster, it is a great honor to serve as the Centennial planning chair.

As we commemorate the 100th anniversary of this great institution in 2015, we do so with great pride—pride in where we have been, pride in where we are now, and pride in where we are going.

Webster's Centennial celebration is inclusive of all colleges, schools, and Webster locations and inspires diverse audiences to recommit to Webster's mission and vision.

Illuminate the Way Home is a central theme for our Centennial, as we invite people to come home to Webster—no matter where "home" might be to them. In this, our Centennial year, we reinvigorate and energize audiences around the world to recommit to Webster University's noble mission of transforming students for global citizenship and individual excellence.

I have a great deal of gratitude for this amazing university—founded so long ago with lofty pursuits to take education to where it is needed in the world. I have personally benefited greatly by the values espoused by the Sisters of Loretto and am so pleased to see them live on today in the hearts and minds of Webster's faculty, staff, students, and alumni, and in our communities. We are linked together by a bond that transcends time and generations. We are and always have been entrepreneurial, fearless, and passionately dedicated to helping others.

Elizabeth Robb, '65
Centennial Planning Chair

FROM LOCAL COLLEGE TO WORLDWIDE UNIVERSITY

The story of Webster University is the story of the human spirit, a spirit constantly dreaming of a better tomorrow, persevering through unending challenges, embracing new frontiers, and believing anything is possible with a combination of faith, intellect, hard work, and a helping hand. From humble beginnings in a single building in America's heartland, the Sisters of Loretto guided the young college through its formative years and laid the foundation for the university we see today. In the second half of the 20th century, administrators, trustees, faculty, staff, and alumni worked together to implement a new model of governance which led to growth not only of physical campuses but of innovative programs with a global reach. Webster today boldly claims the world as its classroom and inclusiveness as its lingua franca.

The Courage to Act Produces a Singular College — 3

A Tradition of Inclusive Leadership — 10

The Home Campus Evolves — 23

Reaching Out to Working Adults — 34

Support for Active Military and Veterans — 42

Broadening Perspectives through Global Opportunities — 50

ANNOUNCEMENT

Loretto College and Academy, Webster Groves, Missouri, now nearing completion, will open for classes, under the direction of the Sisters of Loretto, at the Foot of the Cross, Wednesday, September thirteenth, Nineteen Hundred and Sixteen.

The school will comprise three departments: Collegiate, Academic and Preparatory.

Catalogue will be mailed upon application to Mother Superior, Loretto Academy, 3407 Lafayette Avenue, Saint Louis, Missouri; or Mother Superior, Loretto Academy, Kansas City, Missouri.

After August fifteenth address

Mother Superior

Loretto College and Academy,

Webster Groves, Missouri.

The Manchester-Meramec car, which may be taken at the Union Station, passes the door of the Institution, while the Big Bend Road, bounding the College Campus on the south, affords a pleasant means of access by automobile or carriage.

The Missouri Pacific and the Frisco Railroads have stations at Webster Groves and Old Orchard, respectively, within convenient distance of the Institution.

1915 LORETTO COLLEGE OPENS

In the early 1900s, women who wanted a higher education in a Catholic environment had few choices. Most well-known Catholic universities were just open to men, and only a small number of Catholic women's colleges existed in the United States.

In 1915, the Loretto Community, a Catholic order of nuns, agreed to open a college in St. Louis, MO. These dedicated women not only filled a need for higher education for Catholic women of that era, but established a university that would bring learning to tens of thousands of students worldwide over the next 100 years.

The site for the college was the land originally occupied by the Loretto Seminary for Girls, which had opened there in 1898 and closed after a fire in 1904. The sisters chose the abandoned site for Loretto College—the forerunner of Webster University. The school would be one of the first women's colleges west of the Mississippi River.

The college welcomed its first five students, all graduates of Loretto Academy, a boarding school in Kansas City, MO, in the fall of 1915. Classes were held at Loretto in Kansas City during construction of the building now called Webster Hall. A year later, Loretto College opened on September 13 in its new facility. The building has served an important role in the college's operations ever since. Today, Webster Hall houses classrooms, offices, the Winifred Moore Auditorium, and a Welcome Center for prospective students.

One hundred years later, Webster University still embodies the spirit of the Sisters of Loretto: to take education where it is needed, whether it be a city in the Midwest United States or a campus halfway around the world.

The Courage To Act Produces a Singular College

"Today, you may justly look back with satisfaction over the trying task of organizing so great an undertaking, of attempting pioneer work in the field that called for heroic courage and unflagging enthusiasm."

~ *From Rev. Francis V. Corcoran's address at Webster's first commencement*

The Courage To Act Produces a Singular College

FLORENCE WADDOCK, A. B. '19.

In June 1919, the young college reached its first significant milestone when it graduated the inaugural class of Loretto College.

That first commencement featured two graduates: Florence Waddock, who would teach high school English, French and math, and Sr. Ann Francis, a member of the Loretto Community.

Loretto College's first commencement, held June 4, 1919, fulfilled a bold decision by the Sisters of Loretto in 1915 to build the only Catholic college for women within several hundred miles. The sisters developed a liberal education that trained women for careers—a progressive concept in an era when US women first gained the right to vote in 1920.

In later years, the commencement ceremony included ivy planting and the reading of an ivy poem written by a student. Today, Webster's annual main commencement includes over 1,000 graduates from around the world, with over 10,000 in attendance.

1924 RENAMING TO WEBSTER COLLEGE

Sr. Louise Wise

When Loretto College opened in 1915, it joined an array of elementary schools and high school academies operated by the Sisters of Loretto. Often, the young college was confused with two Loretto Academies for girls in St. Louis. That issue was resolved in 1924 when its name was changed to Webster College. The new name was chosen in honor of Webster Groves, the city in which the home campus is located, and in recognition of Benjamin Webster, the previous owner of the land on which the college was built.

Webster cleared another hurdle a year later with accreditation from the North Central Association (NCA), largely through the efforts of Sr. Louise Wise, Webster's dean.

Webster's tradition of academic excellence had been established even then, and the college passed NCA's inspection with high marks. The NCA inspector called the teaching at Webster "superior" and said "he had inspected women's colleges from Maine to the Gulf and never met one better organized and equipped."

NCA unanimously recommended Webster for full accreditation in the spring of 1925, a distinction Webster has held for the past ninety years.

Starting in 1924, Webster published a traditional yearbook called the *Lauretanum*, filled with features found in most other yearbooks, then and now. Although similar in content to its peers, the 1926 *Lauretanum* distinguished itself by winning a national yearbook competition.

But Webster's traditional yearbook changed radically in 1967, a year that saw Webster become a secular college. Webster's students produced the *Non-Yearbook*, a multimedia effort that included cartoons, quotations, and audio recordings of students, faculty, and staff.

The offbeat approach reached its summit in 1968 with the *Webster College Year Box*. As the title implied, a box housed the yearbook's contents. They included a board game, a spinning wheel of photos, a jigsaw puzzle, and posters. The *Year Box* won prizes at the St. Louis Art Directors Annual Awards in 1968, including Best of Show and the Strathmore Paper Award for most creative use of paper.

The 1969 edition, replete with photos and quotations, marked the final yearbook—traditional or otherwise—from Webster University.

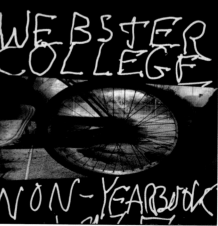

1926 MAY DAY

Today May Day, an important holiday in most of the world, goes largely ignored in the United States. At one time, however, the holiday was celebrated at numerous institutions throughout the nation, including Webster College.

The holiday often includes students performing an intricate dance around a Maypole, and Webster College was no exception. But May Day at Webster also included other features. The *Lauretanum*, Webster's yearbook, first mentions May Day on campus in 1926. The festivities included students electing a queen and her court.

The election of a May queen and her court became an annual fixture at Webster until 1963, when the celebration moved to a hotel and included a spring dance. Citing costs, disinterest, and a belief that electing a queen and her court had no purpose, Webster ended the May Day tradition in 1966.

The Courage To Act Produces a Singular College

On January 11, 1967, a decision was announced that laid the groundwork for today's Webster University. Sr. Jacqueline Grennan, then president of Webster College, announced that Webster would transition from a Catholic college to a secular one. The college would be turned over to a lay board of directors by the Sisters of Loretto, ending their ownership of the school they had operated for just over fifty years. Webster thus became the first Catholic college in US history to become secular.

At the time Webster was one of many Catholic colleges struggling to remain afloat. A third of Catholic colleges founded between 1900 and 1955 failed because of financial shortfalls, declining enrollment and secular competition. Financial issues in particular vexed Webster. The Sisters of Loretto were unsure they had the funds or the faculty to continue operating Webster.

It was also an era when women were reexamining their roles in the church and in society at large. For Grennan, the issue was deeply personal. One of Grennan's conclusions, she said, was that "the very nature of higher education is opposed to juridical control by the church." That belief meant to her that she could not keep her religious vow of obedience to the church as Webster's president. At the same time as the Sisters of Loretto were asking the Vatican's permission for the transfer of ownership, Grennan was requesting that she be released from her religious vows. Both requests were granted, and a new era had begun for Grennan and for Webster.

The college's new lay board of directors met weekly to address "a wide range of problems, including debt, tenure, upgrading student living quarters, and others," remembered Sanford Zimmerman, chairman of the lay board and a well-known businessman. Thanks to their efforts and Grennan's leadership, the college was able to weather the storms caused by societal changes and financial pressures. This new group of leaders would help Webster set out on an ambitious path on its way to becoming the university it is today.

First lay board
Front row, l-r:
Peg Jostedt, Sr.
Rose Maureen Sanders,
Sanford J. Zimmerman, Sr.
Jacqueline Grennan,
Sr. Francetta Barberis,
Lee M. Liberman;
second row, l-r:
Francis V. Lloyd Jr.,
Leonard Hornbein,
Michael Witunski,
Jane Hart, Joseph Kelly;
back row:
George D. O'Neill

Sanford
Zimmerman

Jacqueline
Grennan and
a student

1916–2015 PRESIDENTS

A Tradition of Inclusive Leadership

1. **Mother M. Dolorine Powers**
   President, 1916-1919

2. **Mother M. Edith Loughran**
   President, 1919-1925

3. **Mother M. Linus Maier**
   President, 1925-1931

4. **Dr. George F. Donovan**
   President, 1931-1950

5. **Sr. Mariella Collins**
   President, 1950-1958

6. **Sr. Francetta Barberis**
   President, 1958-1965

7. **Jacqueline Grennan Wexler**
   President, 1965-69

8. **Dr. Leigh Gerdine**
   President, 1970-1990

9. **Dr. Daniel H. Perlman**
   President, 1990-1994

10. **Dr. Richard S. Meyers**
    President, 1994-2008

11. **Dr. Elizabeth (Beth) J. Stroble**
    President, 2009-

1 2 3

4 5

A Tradition of Inclusive Leadership

6 7 8

9 10 11

11

A Tradition of Inclusive Leadership

Marta Brown

Including student voices in the affairs of Webster University is a tradition almost as old as the school itself.

While known as Loretto College, the school experimented with a form of student government from 1920-22. The forerunner of today's Student Government Association began in 1927, three years after Loretto College became Webster College. Students meeting on the night of Nov. 8, 1927, adopted a constitution and by-laws for a student association made up of the entire all-female enrollment of 157 students. On Nov. 28, the Webster College Student Association elected Marta Brown as its first president.

The Student Association's purpose was "to further students' welfare by cooperation with the faculty and to maintain the ideals of morality, scholarship and loyalty upon which Webster College was founded."

Student inclusiveness at Webster College didn't end there. The powers of the Student Association also included electing 10 of the 12 members of the Student Council, which sponsored all but religious student activities. Today, the Student Government Association advocates on behalf of students in university affairs, charters and funds student organizations, supports student organization leadership, and funds large-scale organization events and student trips.

1967 SHARED GOVERNANCE

Faculty involvement in the governance of Webster took on a very active role in the wake of the university's transition to a secular institution. President Jacqueline Grennan formed a Consultative Committee which included faculty to assist with decision-making during the transition and to help prepare a policy handbook on governmental structure to be used after the lay board assumed responsibility.

A Faculty Constituent Assembly composed of all faculty soon followed. Members elected a steering committee (later to be known as the Faculty Executive Committee) to represent the faculty in administrative matters. This organization helped the faculty have a strong voice during this era of great change.

The tremendous growth in the size and complexity of Webster University over the past fifty years has been accompanied by the increased involvement of both faculty and staff in its governance. Today faculty and staff work with administrators to provide effective leadership for the university. Those voices come from two organizations: the Faculty Senate and the Webster Staff Alliance, whose president and chair serve on the eleven-member Administrative Council with the university's top-level administrators. The Administrative Council is led by the President.

Founded in 1996, the Faculty Senate consists of sixteen members who represent faculty opinion to university leadership and who are empowered to decide issues important to the faculty. Senate members are elected from the 200-plus members of the Faculty Assembly, which represents the colleges and schools that make up Webster University.

To represent all staff members to Webster's leadership, the Webster Staff Alliance was formed in 1990. The Staff Alliance also promotes professional development opportunities for Webster University's staff.

Conversations with the Faculty, from left: Bob Strowbridge, Barbara Polk, Peter Sargent, Helen O'Brien Sheahan

A Tradition of Inclusive Leadership

1983

WORLDWIDE DIRECTORS' CONFERENCES

"Better together through a stronger Webster."

That theme from 2011's event aptly captures the spirit of Webster University's Worldwide Directors' conferences. The conferences are opportunities for directors from Webster's extended campus network to add their voices to the future direction of the school.

Held nearly every year for the past three decades, the conferences bring the directors together with the university's leaders at Webster's home campus in St. Louis. The directors interact with Webster's leaders, participate in workshops on a variety of topics, and return to their campuses with a uniform vision for the future of higher education in general and Webster University in particular.

Beth Russell and Nancy Hellerud

Critical to Webster University's success through the years has been the presence of exceptional top-level administrators. Together with the presidents, these individuals have provided crucial leadership through both bountiful and challenging times.

The position of provost was first created at Webster in 1986. Dr. Joseph P. Kelly, a vice-president who had been at Webster since the late 1960s, served as the university's first provost until 1991. Former religious studies professor and dean Dr. William J. Duggan followed from 1991-95, including a term as interim president. The provost position was replaced in 1995 by the executive vice president and vice president for academic affairs position, which was held by Dr. Neil J. George until 2008, when he became interim president. Dr. George became the university's first, and so far only, chancellor in 2009.

In 2010, President Beth Stroble created the new position of provost, senior vice president, and chief operating officer with the goal of aligning academics and operations in one portfolio. Dr. Julian Z. Schuster was named to this position as the number two executive, assuming the roles of chief academic officer and chief operating officer.

As chief academic officer, Dr. Schuster is responsible for providing leadership and strategic direction for the university's academic mission, academic programs and support units, faculty, and research and grants. As chief operating officer, he is responsible for ensuring that operations, such as finance, facilities, information technology, and enrollment management, are aligned with the academic endeavors to ensure a seamless experience for students.

"Webster University has always been an innovator," Schuster said. "That innovation will accelerate in its next century and we will remain on the leading edge of global-based experiential education. We are leading the way in sharing our global capacity with others through quality academic programs and national and global partnerships."

A Tradition of Inclusive Leadership

1992 LEADERSHIP BY DEANS OF SCHOOLS AND COLLEGES

The rapid growth of the university during the last quarter of the 20th century required a new organizational model of inclusive leadership. Presidents Daniel Perlman and Richard Meyers and their administrations built that model in the 1990s. They reorganized Webster from departments with academic vice presidents to individual schools and colleges, each led by its own dean.

First to form was the School of Business and Management in 1992. The rapid growth of information technology prompted the school to change its name to Business & Technology in 1995. Under the leadership of Dr. Neil George, then executive vice president for academic affairs, following in rapid succession were the

College of Fine Arts, the College of Arts & Sciences, the School of Education, and the School of Communications.

The reorganization confirmed a far-sighted leadership decision that would, as was said in 1994, "provide an organizational structure to support and encourage continued growth in standards, focused promotional efforts in all areas, and related curriculum developments." The structure of two colleges and three schools serves Webster well to this day as the colleges and schools continue to evolve, most recently in the creation of two divisions in the College of Arts & Sciences: Liberal Arts and Professional Programs.

L-R: Peter Sargent, Eric Rothenbuhler, Brenda Fyfe, David Wilson, and Benjamin Akande

1994 WEBSTERLEADS AND STUDENT AMBASSADORS

At Webster University, students are included in important leadership roles, thanks to WebsterLEADS and Webster University Student Ambassadors.

WebsterLEADS is the culmination of a twenty-year-old undergraduate program to develop campus leaders. Originally called the Student Leadership Program at its birth in 1994, WebsterLEADS has grown from a handful of participants to more than 250 students at Webster's global campuses. The program immerses students in five areas: classes, retreats, professional development workshops, service learning projects and practical experience. Students completing the curriculum receive the WebsterLEADS Leadership Certificate and the confidence to lead from wherever they are.

The Student Ambassadors are a diverse group of students who are chosen to represent the university. Originally organized as the Student Alumni Association to connect students with alumni, the Student Ambassadors serve as the official student representatives for Webster University's President's Office and Office of Advancement. They can be found greeting and

Student Ambassadors, 2013-14

conversing with guests at university-sponsored events; providing student perspectives to government officials, donors and dignitaries who visit campus; and representing the university at external conferences. To be accepted into the program, Student Ambassadors must meet rigorous academic standards, demonstrate credibility, enthusiasm, initiative and leadership, and pass an interview. The result is a cadre of students who showcase the quality and diversity of the student body and who promote pride in and understanding of Webster University.

A Tradition of Inclusive Leadership

1997 DELEGATES' AGENDA

"The Delegates' Agenda has become a really important part of student life as student leaders have found a way to effectively advocate for change on campus."

~ *Associate Vice President and Dean of Students Ted Hoef*

Students have had a voice in the affairs of Webster University since its early days. Today student involvement takes many forms, including one begun in 1997 and thought to be unique among colleges and universities: the Delegates' Agenda.

Twice annually, delegates from student clubs and organizations and the Student Government Association convene to collect ideas and prioritize them. About a dozen delegates research the top ideas and propose realistic action on them at a meeting with the president, provost, vice presidents, deans, and any interested students, faculty, and staff. Within two to four weeks, the university administration

reports back to the delegates on how each topic will be addressed.

The Delegates' Agenda has improved many aspects of student life, including student housing, on-campus food, parking, facilities, and academic, sustainability, and diversity issues.

Through this process, students and administrators work together to improve Webster University. Administrators receive vital input from students' perspectives, and students develop leadership skills and gain invaluable experience in effecting positive change. The Delegates' Agenda is a prime example of putting students first at Webster University.

2012 WORKING GROUPS

"We will show true teamwork — where every move that is made relates to stretch goals, where every hand off and pick up is executed with precision and skill and intent to achieve great things."

~ Provost, Senior Vice President and Chief Operating Officer Julian Z. Schuster

Where Webster University wants to go, and how it will get there, will be decided not by a few administrators, but by every faculty member, staff member, and student who wants to get involved.

One major opportunity to do that was provided by working groups established in 2012. The working groups focused on seven areas vital to Webster University's future: recruitment and enrollment; retention; organizational realignment; science, technology, engineering, math and medicine; diversity and inclusion; external outreach and engagement; and policies, procedures and shared governance.

More than 300 individuals joined working groups to review current practices, search for better ones, and recommend changes. These recommendations informed a new strategic plan as faculty, students, staff and administrators worked together to map the direction for Webster University.

"I'm honored to work for an institution that values the voices of its stakeholders – faculty, staff, students, and community. Webster's commitment to an engaged institutional culture is demonstrated by its investment in the GLA and other collaborative ventures."

~ Linda Dahlgren, Development Officer, Foundation & Government Grants

A Tradition of Inclusive Leadership

Scholars throughout history have debated what leadership means and how it is acquired. But it is agreed that leadership must be cultivated in any organization seeking excellence.

Webster University took that lesson to heart in 2012 when President Beth Stroble and Provost Julian Schuster created the Global Leadership Academy. The academy helps faculty and staff develop the ability to lead from where they are, no matter what the level or the job.

All full-time and part-time faculty and staff are eligible. The academy selects fifteen to twenty applicants annually to participate as fellows. In addition to online work throughout the year, they meet in person for three weeklong sessions—at the home campus, at an international campus, and at military and metro campuses—to learn how to incorporate specific elements of leadership into their work.

"At the core of the academy is empowerment of the university's people," says Laura Wainz, a 2012 fellow. "We have great people working here, and the academy encourages us to step up and be a vibrant part of the university."

2013 GLA Cohort

L-R: Linda Dahlgren, Jade Venditte, and Kelly Lyon

2012 GLA Cohort

U.S. ARMY COMMAND AND GENERAL STAFF COLLEGE

President Stroble and Provost Schuster

Stephanie Schroeder

Sr. Carlann Herman

1928 FIRST HOME CAMPUS EXPANSION

Webster's enrollment doubled during the 1920s, reaching 177 in 1929. In response, Webster embarked on its first expansion since the completion of the school's original building, Webster Hall, in 1916. On September 30, 1928, Loretto Hall opened as a new residence for students who had been living in the adjacent Webster Hall. Webster built the four-story Loretto Hall at a cost of $325,000 to house 196 students and twelve Sisters of Loretto. The new building allowed Webster Hall to be used strictly for academic and administrative purposes.

Sr. Mariella Collins, who formally became Webster's president in 1950, took note of the rising tide of "Baby Boomers" following World War II and called for additional student housing. In 1957, Webster received a $655,000 government loan to fund an addition to Loretto Hall. The new five-story addition opened in 1959 with room for 116 students and a ground-level cafeteria with a capacity for 360. A "name-the-wing contest" for students and faculty resulted in the new addition being christened Maria Hall.

LORETTO HALL
STUDENTS' RESIDENCE HALL
WEBSTER COLLEGE

Home Campus Evolves

1960 SECOND HOME CAMPUS EXPANSION

Sr. Francetta Barberis brought with her a reputation as a builder when she became Webster College's president in 1958. Webster quickly learned why.

Barberis, who had led a major expansion while at Loretto Academy in El Paso, Texas, called for a fund drive to bankroll additional scholarships, higher faculty salaries, and new facilities at Webster. Her plan bore its first fruit in 1960 with a clever exchange of property with the Episcopal Church to acquire the Thompson House, which Webster renovated and converted into today's music building. Four years later, Webster built the experimental College School for teacher training, which serves today as the visual arts studios. That same year ground was broken for the Loretto-Hilton Center for the Performing Arts, which was completed in 1966.

The Thompson House and The College School marked Webster's first steps across Big Bend Boulevard. Further strides on that side of the road east of the Thompson House came with the purchase of the Dooley House in 1985, renamed the Pearson House in 1987 after former English department faculty member Sr. Deborah Pearson, and the Howe House, now the H. Sam Priest Center for International Studies, in 1989.

Sr. Francetta Barberis

Pearson House

Sr. Deborah Pearson

Thompson House

H. Sam Priest Center

1966 LORETTO-HILTON CENTER FOR THE PERFORMING ARTS

"The Loretto-Hilton Center's aim is to get our students and our faculty involved in the real work of professional theatre as opposed to the mock-heroic world of the educational theatre."

~ *Sr. Jacqueline Grennan, then Executive Vice President*

The unique nature of Webster University's renowned Conservatory of Theatre Arts—training ground for several Tony and Emmy Award-winners—exists thanks to the visionary efforts that culminated in the creation of the Loretto-Hilton Center for the Performing Arts in 1966.

Sr. Marita Michenfelder (later known as Marita Woodruff) planted the seeds after becoming head of Webster's Theatre Department in 1957. A year later, Michenfelder and fellow faculty member Sr. Frances Kenoyer asked Webster to develop a fine arts center. This was a bold proposal for a program that had just ten students in 1957. Nevertheless, by 1961, enrollment had grown to thirty. That same year, Michenfelder, together with theatre instructor Wayne Loui, started Theatre Impact, an outdoor company that featured Webster students and professional actors working together.

The success of Theatre Impact gave new life to the idea of a year-round fine arts center on Webster's campus. President Sr. Francetta Barberis and Vice President Sr. Jacqueline Grennan successfully solicited financial support from Conrad Hilton, founder of Hilton Hotels, who as a young boy had been educated by the Sisters of Loretto.

With Hilton providing three-fourths of the $1.9 million that was eventually needed, the Loretto-Hilton Center became the first in the United States to serve as home to a professional acting company, the Repertory Theatre of St. Louis, and an undergraduate theatre arts department. The Rep, as it came to be called, and Webster's Conservatory of Theatre Arts remain partners today, pleasing passionate playgoers while grooming a new generation of Webster University theatre students. In 1976, the Loretto-Hilton Center also became home to the Opera Theatre of Saint Louis.

Conrad Hilton with
Sr. Jacqueline Grennan

Sverdrup Complex

Webster Village Apartments

1988 THIRD HOME CAMPUS EXPANSION

In the 1980s, Webster embarked on its biggest construction boom in twenty years. The effort demanded careful planning and multiple revisions to gain local government support. The work paid off with construction of the Sverdrup Complex, the University Center, and Webster Village Apartments.

Named for Gen. Leif J. Sverdrup, whose fundraising helped save Webster in the early 1970s, the Sverdrup Complex opened in 1988 at a cost of $6.5 million. Today, the building is home to the School of Communications.

While the Sverdrup Complex helped solve classroom shortages, Webster lacked a student union and athletic facilities. That ended when the $5.5 million University Center opened a few hundred feet from Sverdrup in 1992. The University Center provides a wealth of services to students on the St. Louis campus.

Meanwhile, the campus had not seen any new housing in almost forty years until Webster Village Apartments welcomed residents in 1998. The attractive complex for 280 residents offers a clubhouse and swimming pool, all just a short walk from class.

University Center

2001 FOURTH HOME CAMPUS EXPANSION

If one were to list issues common to most US colleges, shortages of parking and on-campus housing would be at or near the top. These issues helped propel Webster University to embark on the fourth expansion of the home campus: the opening of the Garden Park Plaza parking garage and the East and West Halls.

Parking on the home campus was already at a premium, and the upcoming construction of the Emerson Library (scheduled to open in 2003) on the site of a parking lot promised to make the problem even worse. Webster University's solution: go vertical.

The university proposed to build a four-story parking garage on Garden Avenue, two blocks east of the site for the new library. The garage, called Garden Park Plaza, opened in 2001, just before the lot on Edgar Road closed for library construction.

The $6.5 million facility provided much-needed space for more than just vehicles. In addition to accommodating 675 cars, Garden Park Plaza became the new home for the Department of Public Safety, a greatly expanded bookstore, and the Academic Advising and Career Planning and Development Centers, all on the ground level.

Meanwhile, Webster University met the rising demand for on-campus housing by building East and West Halls on Hazel Avenue near Garden Park Plaza and Emerson Library. The 343-bed residence halls cost $15.4 million and opened in September 2006.

Webster University completed its fourth wave of construction on the home campus with a new building, which opened in 2007 next to the Loretto-Hilton Center for the Performing Arts. The facility is home to the Community Music School of Webster University, which the university acquired from the St. Louis Symphony in 2001.

Emerson Library

East and West Halls

Community Music School building

Joseph Roberts

2012 EAST ACADEMIC BUILDING

The $29 million, 94,000 square-foot EAB incorporates a striking design by noted architect Robert A.M. Stern. This signature building features the most up-to-date instruction design and technology and includes thirty-one classrooms, ten large computer labs, forty-eight offices, and two large lobbies.

Home to the George Herbert Walker School of Business & Technology, the EAB is one of only thirty-one buildings in St. Louis to receive Gold Leadership in Energy and Environmental Design certification from the U.S. Green Building Council for environmentally friendly design and energy-saving features. The council recognized EAB's numerous sustainability features, including native plant rain gardens, vegetative green roofs, and an energy-saving vapor barrier envelope.

The EAB was named "Facility of the Year" by the International Facility Management Association for innovation in design and construction.

March 28, 2012, marked a key moment in the life of Webster University: the dedication of the East Academic Building (EAB). The EAB was the first new classroom building at Webster's home campus in nearly thirty years. It resolved a critical classroom shortage that had been addressed for many years by leasing space at Webster Groves High School. The building quickly earned a place as a premier facility.

1932 SATURDAY CLASSES

Webster University's weekend, night, and online classes for working professionals owe their start to a Webster president who was a non-traditional student himself.

George Donovan, who taught history at Webster College while studying for a doctorate degree at St. Louis University, became Webster's first lay president in 1931. During his seventeen-year tenure, Donovan brought the real world to Webster's students by introducing courses on current events and guest lecturers who addressed topics of the time.

It was in that spirit that Webster catered to non-traditional students with the introduction of Saturday classes in 1932. In keeping with Webster's all-female enrollment, they were open to business and professional women, Webster residents, and nuns.

Under Donovan's successor, Sr. Mariella Collins, Webster expanded its offerings to non-traditional students. The first summer credit courses appeared in 1954. Webster's first evening classes started in February 1955 with non-credit courses for alumnae in beginning art and home economics.

1970 LAW ENFORCEMENT EDUCATION PROGRAM

President Richard Meyers and Chief of Police Clarence Harmon

Just three years after becoming secular, Webster expanded its efforts to meet the needs of non-traditional students when it opted in 1970 to participate in the Law Enforcement Education Program (LEEP). Sponsored by the U.S. Department of Justice, LEEP encouraged higher education for law enforcement officials and individuals planning to work in law enforcement by offering loans and grants to help with tuition.[1]

LEEP at Webster focused on increasing professionalism among law enforcement officials. For example, offerings included a course intended to "help policemen to understand better their role in the life of the community and to understand community behavior patterns," according to a Webster news release. Participants in LEEP included Clarence Harmon, a future chief of police and mayor of St. Louis.

Webster's participation in LEEP demonstrated Webster's emphasis on higher education for working adults—a commitment that continues today.

1972 FIRST METRO CAMPUS IN KANSAS CITY

"Webster students have so much opportunity here in Kansas City. Webster students know that they will receive high-quality academic programs and personal attention."

~ *Midwest Metropolitan Region Director Cass Butler*

Webster University in Kansas City, MO, holds the distinction of being Webster's first metro campus. It was founded in 1972 to fill a specific need in the community.

Srs. Eleanor Craig and Marlene Spero taught math at Kansas City's Loretto Academy in the early 1970s. They brought Webster's successful master of arts in teaching program for elementary educators to an eager audience. "Many students were inner-city teachers seeking new ideas," Spero said.[2]

Craig and Spero, the first faculty of the Kansas City campus, taught classes at night and during the summer. The duo maintained the program's emphasis on nine-week courses delivered by practicing professionals.

More than forty years later, the Kansas City location carries on that work to more than 350 students and continues to meet community needs with innovative degrees such as an MA in education and innovation: education for global sustainability. In January 2015, the Kansas City campus moved to its new, improved facilities.

1973 MA PROGRAM

"For some, the program will serve as enrichment before final career decisions are made; for others it may represent a method for entry into a second or third career; for still others it may serve as a stocktaking of the educational worth of life and work experience."

~ *William Duggan, from an early 1970s proposal for a master of arts program for working adults*

Thousands of working adults enroll each term in Webster University's once-a-week, nine-week graduate courses. The success of that concept stems from a simple request, and a faculty member determined to see it through.

In 1973, the Missouri Parole Officers Association requested a master's degree to advance their professional skills. At the time, Webster offered only a master's in education.

Dr. William Duggan, a religion professor who nearly twenty years later would become university provost, was up for the challenge.

Duggan had already worked with others at Webster to design a graduate program that would allow individual students to set up their own curriculum—an ideal concept for working professionals. When the Missouri Parole Officers Association asked for Webster's help, Duggan saw how the individualized program design concept could be extended to entire groups.

The program launched in the summer of 1973 with thirty students. Enrollment skyrocketed as the program added courses and off-site locations. More than 3,800 students were participating by the end of spring 1976, laying the foundation for today's graduate programs for working adults at Webster University.

1975 DOWNTOWN ST. LOUIS CAMPUS

Webster University's commitment to higher education for working adults includes taking that education to where they work . . . and what better place to do that than downtown in Webster's home city, St. Louis?

That rationale led to Webster's decision to open a campus in downtown St. Louis in 1975. From those beginnings in the Boatmen's Bank Building, Webster moved to the Lammert Building in 1986 and to the Old Post Office in 2006. Today, the Old Post Office is part of Webster's Gateway Campus, along with the Arcade Building.

The campus brings Webster's first-class education to a revitalized downtown. Primarily a commercial center when Webster opened its doors there in the mid-1970s, downtown St. Louis and adjacent neighborhoods have been transformed into a living area that has grown from about 800 residents in 2000 to about 14,000 today.[3] Webster offers courses in more than a dozen degrees downtown, making that campus a prime example of honoring Webster's commitment to educating adults where they work—and live.

1975 METRO CAMPUSES

"To help our students succeed, we must expand their access to all levels of education."

~ *Provost, Senior Vice President and Chief Operating Officer Julian Z. Schuster*

Following the successful introduction of its first metro campus in Kansas City in 1972, Webster University made higher education accessible to additional working adults by opening more than twenty-five metro campuses in the United States.

One of the latest came in 2013 when Webster opened a metro campus in San Antonio, Texas, building on Webster's long-time presence at nearby Fort Sam Houston and Lackland and Randolph Air Force Bases. The San Antonio metro campus currently offers a weekend MBA program and master of arts degrees in the areas of business, management, and counseling.

Besides opening new campuses, Webster makes continual investments in its current ones, including moving long-standing campuses to new facilities. Two recent relocations included the Charleston and Columbia, South Carolina campuses, which continue to expand educational access in these growing metropolitan areas.

"These new locations epitomize our strategic commitment to investing in educational experiences of our students at metropolitan campuses," said Provost Julian Schuster. An additional benefit came in 2014 with the establishment of a partnership with BlueCross BlueShield of South Carolina (BCBS). The partnership provides discounted tuition for BCBS South Carolina employees enrolled at Webster's campuses—another example of Webster making higher education more accessible to working adults.

"More and more employers are recognizing the importance of lifelong learning and how it helps not only their workers but also their workplace. Webster's cohorts are a proven success and the best way to make education accessible to a company's greatest asset — its employees."

~ Chief of the Office of Corporate Partnerships and Dean of the George Herbert Walker School of Business & Technology Benjamin Ola. Akande, 2014

In 1990, Webster University began one of its most successful programs for working adults: corporate cohorts. The corporate cohorts initiative made the pursuit of a college degree convenient and affordable by bringing classes to the employee's workplace at a discounted rate. Employees were able to progress through a degree program as a single group, or cohort, in on-site classes.

Southwestern Bell was the first corporation to partner with Webster. Since its inception, the corporate cohorts program has grown to numerous partnerships with corporations seeking to better prepare their employees for career growth.

A typical example is Webster's partnership with BJC HealthCare in St. Louis. BJC employees pursue master's degrees in nursing or business administration. Since the partnership began in 2006, more than 100 BJC employees have completed their MBAs through the program.

Said Lisa Cook, a graduate of the Webster MBA program at BJC: "Webster has been phenomenal, supplying our cohort with brilliant instructors and professors who are caring and really enjoy their profession. The fact that I had the opportunity to go to class with fellow BJC employees was an added bonus."

"Webster University has been the university anchor for downtown St. Louis for forty years. This expansion marks the next phase of our partnership with the city and those who live and work downtown."

~ *President Elizabeth (Beth) J. Stroble*

Webster University's forty-year mission to bring higher education to working adults in downtown St. Louis took a giant step forward when President Stroble and Provost Schuster established the Gateway Campus in 2014.

The Gateway Campus includes existing space in the Old Post Office, Webster's downtown home since 2006, with new facilities across Olive Street in the renovated Arcade Building.

The Old Post Office and the Arcade Building embody Webster's vision to be a leading partner in the renovation of landmark sites. Both buildings are listed in the National Register of Historic Places. Webster is the lead anchor tenant in the Arcade restoration that will include classrooms, offices, a coffeehouse, an art museum, and an auditorium.

Plans for the Arcade Building also call for 282 lofts and apartments, making the Gateway Campus truly a place where working adults—and potential Webster students—will not only learn but also live.[4]

Reaching Out to Working Adults

Support for Active Military and Veterans

Loretto College had been open in Webster Groves for barely six months when the United States entered World War I in April 1917. But that didn't stop the college and its tiny student body from beginning Webster University's tradition of supporting the military.

Although enrollment during the war years of 1917-18 peaked at just twenty-five, students at the all-female college participated in formal and informal efforts to help the United States and its allies win the war.

The college held at least two events in support of the war effort. Loretto College staged a patriotic pageant, *The Drawing of the Sword*, in the auditorium on June 2, 1918. Proceeds from tickets, priced at fifty cents each, went to the Webster Groves Chapter of the Red Cross.[5] The auditorium also served as the site for a Catholic Women's War League rally in November 1918, which gathered pledges totaling $1,000.

Florence Waddock, the college's first graduate, wrote an article for the *Lorettine* describing war support efforts. Meanwhile, students and faculty provided aid that went directly to the military by knitting socks and headgear for the troops.

KNIGHTS OF COLUMBUS, PATRIOTS.

Since the day that our Country's state of war was officially announced, patriotism in its various aspects, has been the uppermost consideration of the general public. At first the idea of our being at war was too vague to bring forth any results, but as the days passed a mysterious feeling took possession of man, seized him and grew upon him, a feeling that gave him courage to realize what war means, what it demands from him. What was this feeling? Whence did it come? It was the feeling of country first, the feeling that fired the patriots of '76, that has made the American forget his own interests to help a weaker brother in so many of our wars that have followed. It was Patriotism and it came from the loyal hearts of America's sons.

This noble virtue has various degrees, from the first evinced by those who are willing to leave position, pleasure, wealth, home to aid the cause with their lives, down to the little school girl who contributes to the cause by her knitting and Red Cross work. Each and all do their "bit", and the cause is nobler when we consider that our boys are giving their lives and mothers their heart's blood, not to defend their own country, but to aid others who in distress, have called upon them. But not less patriotic than our noble soldier lads are those who give time and labor to the spiritual and temporal welfare of our country's defenders. Among these are the Knights of Columbus who are proving themselves true patriots in their great movement to better the conditions for the soldiers in camp, the great movement of the "War Encampment Fund", which will provide full spiritual and recreational facilities. The work is certainly good for the purpose, the means employed and the end in view are indeed praise-worthy.

The Knights of Columbus propose to provide a hundred recreation halls fully equipped, which will be open to all American soldiers regardless of creed; to supply extra chaplains so that every thousand Catholic boys can have the services of a priest; to place trained secretaries in charge

of the various halls who will be personally interested in the welfare of the soldiers, who will promote for their amusement athletics and indoor activities. The halls will afford clean sport and counter act temptations. They will contain libraries where Uncle Sam's boys can indulge in good, wholesome, up-to-date reading for diversion or for educational purposes. They propose to safeguard the morals of our men. For our nation's endurance in this strenuous combat, men strong morally are just as essential, if not more so, than men strong physically. If the morals of the men are wholesome when they enter the camp, they will remain so; if they are weak, they will be so protected by the clean environment that they will be daily strengthened. With sound morals our soldiers will live nobly, fight courageously and if need be, die with honor.

This project of the Knights of Columbus should meet with the favor and esteem of all American citizens, for we see the cause is truly worthy and the means necessary to bring about this result is being encouraged by the government and promoted by high officials of the Church, men prominent in this truly Catholic Order. For it is a means, athletics and healthy recreation, that is sane and efficient. Towards the carrying out of this truly patriotic scheme, the Knights are bending their united efforts, and though the term "slacker" has been much over-worked, he who fails to co-operate with these workers, is a "slacker" indeed. If a citizen cannot aid his country with personal service he should at least offer his "bit" in a financial way. And what if this does entail a sacrifice? Can we find a more worthy cause? If this type of "slacker" had a son, brother or dear one in the United States service, would he look with disfavor on the project? Indeed, no, he would be among the first to give aid. Why should he not think of his neighbor's son, brother or friend, and act in this noble cause with an unselfish motive, help to better the condition of those who are so nobly giving their all for the nation? To meet the demand of the sum imposed upon the Knights has entailed from some a severe strain upon an already over-taxed income, from others the mere giving of surplus capital, but both deserve our admiration. How do we feel towards those who have failed to support the movement? Archbishop Glennon expresses it fully for us when he says: "If they can and won't come

to the assistance of those who are working for such a noble end, they are certainly disloyal to their country".

What could be more thoroughly patriotic than to keep our soldier boys, clean, manly Americans; to provide means that they may live right and die with all the consolations of their holy religion? The Young Men's Christian Association is working towards much the same end, but they cannot afford Catholic soldiers the spiritual comfort which is always needed in time of trial. And when has a time of trial been more in evidence than it is right now? Trials of every sort beset the soldier. He must be fitted to live right and be prepared to die happily as well as heroically. Could a soldier die nobly who had lived ignobly? No, if we are to have true defenders of our country's integrity, we must have noble men. Our soldiers must lead clean, sane lives measured by the standard of true manhood. By the providing of Chaplains for every thousand soldiers, our priests will have opportunity for a great mission; our Catholic boys, to be examples and ideals for those of the less fortunate sects who have not the same high standard of belief; the difficulties of camp life and service will be easier to meet, death, if it comes will be robbed of half its awfulness for the consolations of religion will bring peace and confidence.

The government invited the Knights of Columbus to provide this spiritual care of the Catholic soldiers. No other organization in the Church was so well-fitted to supply such a timely need, and no other could attempt it with more more energy and enthusiasm than these truly Catholic Knights have shown. Their unity and co-operation will bring success to this great undertaking, the perfecting of our soldiers. The work is noble, their motive is high and the means of attaining the desired end commendable, therefore, in as far as the Knights of Columbus have for the end of the great endeavor the making of efficient soldiers for Uncle Sam, they are in the true sense of the word Patriots, and could anything but success be looked for from these modern Knights whose every movement has for its motive. "For God and Country!"

FLORENCE WADDOCK, Junior.

George Donovan

1941 HOME FRONT ACTIVITIES, WORLD WAR II

"Webster is fighting in her way because she is a part of an America to be fought for. It proved in a way that a girls' college is more fully conscious of what this war means than some would believe. It gave each of us a thrill, knowing that our brothers and our friends, who are fighting a more physical fight, have not been left to battle alone."

~ Webster College student newspaper editorial, June 1, 1945

World War II engulfed the globe on a scope and scale not seen before or since. The conflict involved forty nations and cost an estimated sixty million lives from 1939 to 1945.[6] Winning the war required an all-out effort by military and civilians in the United States.

Webster College proved equal to the challenge.

Soon after America's entry into the war in December 1941, Webster students worked during Christmas vacation to register civil defense volunteers. Starting with the early months of the war, students donated blood.

Greater efforts followed. In 1943, Webster's students raised $80,000 in war bonds; their work was rewarded with having a P-51 Mustang fighter plane called *The Spirit of Webster College*. A year later, the students sold $300,000 in war bonds, and a B-17 Flying Fortress bomber was named *Webster College.* In 1945, the students raised an astonishing $500,000 in war bonds, resulting in the christening of a Victory-class cargo vessel called *Webster Victory.*

Webster's people served, too. At least twenty Webster students joined the military during the war. Webster's service to the nation extended to the postwar era, when President George Donovan accepted an invitation from the government in 1948 to work as civilian administrator and chief of education in the United States zone of occupation in Germany. Sr. Mariella Collins became temporary president, a role that became permanent in 1950.

1968 VAULT

"I have received a number of proposals for training of veterans for public service type positions. Of all these, the proposal of Webster College is beyond doubt the more foresighted and provocative I have seen."

~ *Director, Transitional Manpower Programs, Department of Defense, Frank McKernan*

Some of the most searing images from the 1960s were those from the Vietnam War and the civil rights movement. While African Americans struggled for equal rights at home, more than 2.5 million US soldiers—many of them African Americans—served in Vietnam.[7]

Two Webster College faculty members conceived of a way to use education to help returning Vietnam veterans and improve conditions for African Americans. Drs. Fred Stopsky, assistant professor of history, and V. Miller Newton, associate professor of social science, developed the Veterans Accelerated Urban Learning for Teaching (VAULT) program in 1968.[8]

VAULT trained veterans to become elementary teachers in inner-city schools. Candidates for VAULT were veterans who otherwise might not have attended college. A high percentage of participants were African Americans who not only taught but served as role models for underprivileged youth. The program was the first of its kind in the United States and would be adopted by several other US colleges and universities.[9]

1974 VETERANS AFFAIRS OFFICE AND FIRST MILITARY LOCATION

As the Vietnam War wound down in the mid-1970s, millions of veterans navigated a sometimes tricky course during their transition to civilian life. Whether it was dealing with lingering trauma or simply applying for benefits they deserved, their need was great.[10] Webster College came to their aid in September 1974 when it opened a Veterans Affairs Office on the St. Louis campus. Students and the public could access a variety of services, ranging from counseling to claims processing.

Impressed with Webster University's tradition of helping active military and veterans, the U.S. Department of Defense invited Webster to be the first university in the country to open a campus on a military base in 1974.

The Fort Sheridan campus near Chicago opened that same year, Webster's first extended campus to be located at a military facility. The campus offered the convenience of on-site graduate courses to base personnel.

Webster's ability to support the military and the popularity of the Fort Sheridan campus motivated a rapid expansion of Webster's partnership with the military. More extended campuses followed that same year at Scott Air Force Base, IL, and Fort Leonard Wood, MO. Today, Webster meets the military's need for on-site degree programs by operating extended campuses on more than thirty military bases.

Support for Active Military and Veterans

47

Support for Active Military and Veterans

"Our mission is to provide unmatched educational programs and unparalleled service to our military."

~ Associate Vice President for Military and Government Programs Brigadier General Mike Callan, USAF (Ret.)

President Stroble and Provost Schuster raised the university's historically strong support of the military to an even higher level in 2013 by establishing the Office of Military Affairs (OMA). Headed by retired Air Force Brigadier General Mike Callan, the OMA coordinates all military-related activity at Webster. Those activities are many and varied, starting with the educational programs Webster delivers at its military campuses to 7,700 military students. Those programs have established Webster as a leader in military education and earned Webster a reputation as military- and veteran-friendly.

The OMA strives to enhance relationships with military branches, strengthen military student services, and expand Webster's military and governmental opportunities.

Highlights include:
- making higher education possible for active military, veterans, and dependents through financial aid such as the Proud to Serve and Mike and Ann Callan scholarships;

- proudly sponsoring events such as Salute to the Troops at Fair St. Louis, the region's largest Independence Day celebration;

- partnering with the Webster University Student Veterans Organization (SVO), established by student veterans to raise awareness and serve as an information source for veterans attending Webster. The SVO is a chapter of the Student Veterans of America.

The OMA builds on a distinguished tradition that includes offering educational programs at military installations since 1974. The success of Webster's mission has been widely recognized. In 2014 alone, Webster was ranked among the best colleges for the military by *U.S. News and World Report*, *GI Jobs* magazine, the *Military Times* and the *Military Advanced Education Guide to Colleges and Universities*.

"Webster University has assisted our military students in making their educational dreams come true," Callan said. "The Office of Military Affairs takes great pride in upholding the standards our university demands and our military students deserve."

1925 TRAVEL ABROAD SCHOLARSHIP

"Growing up in St. Louis, I lived in an insular world. The opportunity to live with people from twenty-five different countries at the Leiden campus and to travel in Europe helped me understand just how much bigger than myself and my little world the international community really was."

~ Jeff Remming (Class of 2000)

Webster University's international emphasis, shown by today's global campuses and opportunities to study abroad through the Webster World Traveler program, is almost as old as the school itself.

Webster welcomed its first international students in 1919, just four years after the school opened. One of them, Marcelle Prévost, later returned from her native France to teach French at Webster. In 1925, Webster began awarding summer scholarships for students to study in Europe.

Internationalism at Webster shifted into high gear in the 1930s and 1940s under President George Donovan. He stressed that teachers as well as students should have opportunities to study abroad. He brought more international students to Webster and inspired on-campus events with a global view.

During Donovan's administration, Webster began a chapter of the International Relations Club in 1931, received national recognition for a Pan-American studies program on campus in 1933, became the first Catholic women's college to hold a League of Nations model assembly in 1934, and had almost 200 faculty and students go abroad or come to Webster from other nations from 1931-1950.

Today, Webster receives national recognition for its study abroad program, ranking sixteenth

among all national US master's degree-granting institutions for sending students abroad. In addition, its faculty mobility program, which enables faculty to teach at Webster's international campuses, is unmatched among its peers. Similarly, the Global Staff Exchange, established in 2003 with funding from an Energizer diversity grant and continued today through university funding, provides staff from Webster's worldwide network of campuses with the opportunity for an international professional development experience.

WEBSTER COLLEGE
WEBSTER GROVES MISSOURI
ART-HISTORY TOUR OF EUROPE
JUNE 3 - JULY 15, 1964
TWA   TWA
Arrangements By STANDARD TRAVEL SERVICE, Inc. ST. LOUIS MO.

1978

"Our daughters went through an inspiring transformation during their undergraduate years at Webster Geneva; their perspective widened, their curiosity brightened, and their values shone through more clearly than ever before."

~ *Michelle and Steve Knight, parents of Webster Geneva students Sarah Knight (Class of 2011) and Stefanie Knight (Class of 2014)*

The genesis of Webster University's network of international campuses can be traced to a conversation between a US ambassador to the United Nations and a Midwest college professor in the mid-1970s.

The ambassador, Francis Dale, told John Rider, a mass communications professor visiting Geneva from Southern Illinois University-Edwardsville (SIUE), about the potential for a Midwest college to establish a campus in Geneva. Learning that there were no English-language colleges in Geneva for the approximately 30,000 English-speaking professionals and their families there, Rider decided to act.

Refusing to take no for an answer when SIUE rejected his proposal for a Geneva extension, Rider obtained permission to present his idea to Webster, where he taught part-time. Agreeing

to Rider's proposal would be a daring and risky decision. Although Webster had met with success with its first extended campuses earlier in the 1970s, all were in the continental United States.

Dr. Leigh Gerdine, Webster's president from 1970 to 1990, had helped stabilize the college's critical financial condition earlier in the 1970s partly through opening those first domestic extended campuses. Gerdine, the board, and faculty decided the next step in bringing Webster's education to where students lived and worked would be outside the United States. And what better location for a first global campus than Geneva, home of the United Nations, numerous international organizations, and multinational corporations?

Webster reached the far-sighted decision to establish its first international campus in Geneva

Julianna Bark-Sandholm

Francesco Arese
Visconti

in 1978. Rider took a two-year sabbatical from SIUE to serve as the first director of Webster's Geneva location.

The Geneva campus quickly met with success, leading Webster to open three more international campuses over the next eight years and to expand the Geneva location. Two buildings that house classrooms, a library, computer labs, and cafeteria opened in 1992. A Living and Learning Center featuring student accommodations, classrooms, offices, a fitness center, and recreation facilities made its debut in 2005.

"At Webster University Geneva, the concept of an international education becomes reality, as over 500 students from over ninety countries come together in a community of learners engaged by faculty representing twenty-five nations," states Dr. Clementina Acedo, Webster Geneva campus director.

1981 VIENNA CAMPUS

Some thirty-five years ago, Webster University came to Vienna by invitation.

Vienna Mayor Leopold Gratz visited Webster University's first international campus in Geneva not long after it opened in 1978. Gratz was so impressed that he asked Webster to become the first American university in Austria.[11] In 1981, Vienna became home to Webster's second international campus, one that thrives today in a breathtaking setting near the center of the Austrian capital.

The student population at Webster Vienna, which today comes from over sixty countries, has grown by nearly fifty percent since the university received Austrian private university accreditation in 2001. Besides having the opportunity to experience the rich cultural offerings of the area, Webster students are in close proximity to numerous multinational businesses and global organizations, including the United Nations. Past internship opportunities have included the *Economist*, International Atomic Energy Association, Caritas, and OPEC.

Attracted by such American-style degrees as a master's in international relations, the growing enrollment at the Vienna campus led to several relocations. With the latest move, President Stroble and Provost Schuster made the strategic decision to move the campus to the heart of Vienna, to the Palais Wenkheim, built in 1826. A newly renovated residential facility to house students is just a short walk from the Palais.

Palais Wenkheim is twice as large as Webster's previous Vienna site and provides the space Webster needs to reach its long-range goal to double the current enrollment of 500.

While the new facility is important to the future of the Vienna campus, Webster's focus remains, as always, on its students.

"For three decades, Webster University has offered a truly global classroom experience in Vienna to students from around the world," President Beth Stroble said. "This expansion in Austria is part of our overall mission of offering a superior American-style education in an environment that fosters creativity and collaboration." "Great students and great faculty deserve great facilities, and our Vienna campus epitomizes that," added Provost Julian Schuster.

Palais Wenkheim

1983 LEIDEN CAMPUS

"At Webster University Leiden, we combine the best of the American educational system with a truly international perspective. We strive to achieve our mission of promoting individual excellence alongside global citizenship."

~ *Leiden Campus Director Jean Paul van Marissing*

Webster University broadened its international footprint by opening its third international campus in Leiden, the Netherlands, in 1983.

The location, just minutes from The Hague, home of the International Criminal Court and the International Court of Justice, was an ideal place to broaden students' perspectives through global opportunities. Webster's Leiden location provides its students with unique insights into the world's justice systems—while being the only American-accredited university in the Netherlands that offers undergraduate and graduate degrees.

The uniqueness of the Leiden campus doesn't end there. Also setting apart the Leiden location is its Global Research Center. The center coordinates academic research projects conducted by faculty and students on sustainability and development. Some of the center's efforts include identifying research needs and linking Webster's research projects with corporations, institutions, governments, and non-governmental organizations.

These activities happen on an intimate campus next to a canal. Just 100 steps from the main building is the Living and Learning Center. The center includes recreation facilities and fifty studio apartments for Webster's students. With an enrollment of about 350, Webster Leiden offers the personalized education that is a signature feature of a Webster education. It also offers a vibrant community locally and within short train rides to major cities such as Amsterdam and Rotterdam.

Broadening Perspectives Through Global Opportunities

L-R: Robert Chamberlain, Lord Mayor of Westminster, Mrs. Terence Mallinson, and President Gerdine

1986

"Attending Webster in London, with its diverse student body, definitely prepared me for my future to work with people from different cultures and backgrounds. Being educated as a global citizen means knowing we are all a part of this one planet, knowing about other countries and other people, respecting their ideals and beliefs, and learning to work as one cohesive group."

~ Katherine Wiley (Class of 2012)

The first decade of Webster's mission to become a global university ended on a resounding note in 1986: the opening of a campus in London, Europe's second-largest city.[12]

Rich in the arts, replete with twenty centuries of history, and with seven million people who speak 200 languages representing a cultural cornucopia, London gives Webster's students a wide-ranging window on the world.

Kelley Atherton, a 2007 Webster University graduate, described how "as a journalism major, I took several media classes while in London, which is a hub of information. I took history classes in one of the oldest civilizations, international relations and political science classes in one of the world's capitals, and literature classes in a culture steeped with classics. My instructors were from all over the world, as were my fellow students, who provided different perspectives to class discussions. I ended up staying another semester in London because I was so enamored with the city."

As Webster University looks to the future, it can point with pride to its thirty-year heritage of offering a quality American-style educational experience in London. "London is a strategic location for Webster University and we are going to continue to be present in that part of the world," said Provost Julian Schuster.

Broadening Perspectives Through Global Opportunities

1992 CENTER FOR INTERNATIONAL EDUCATION

"In learning about others, students learn a lot, or maybe even more, about themselves. When we are studying other peoples' cultures, it's amazing how much it requires us to learn about ourselves."

~ *Director, Center for International Education, Deborah Pierce*

While in the midst of establishing locations abroad, Webster University brought a global perspective to students on the home campus in St. Louis through the Center for International Education (CIE).

Created in 1992, the CIE's mission was "to support and promote internationalization of the curriculum, offer community and extra-curricular education, and provide a link with Webster's international campuses," according to Dr. Daniel Hellinger, professor of history, politics, & international relations and an early director of the center.

The CIE accomplished a major part of its mission in 1994 when it gained approval for an international studies certificate. The undergraduate program includes global components such as international language proficiency, study abroad, and internationally focused courses in multiple disciplines. The center also provides the International Distinction Award to students who have competency in a second language, international field work, and study abroad experience.

The CIE serves as a key resource for Webster faculty, staff, and students by providing information on international fellowships, grants, internships, and other programs. The CIE sponsors numerous globally-focused activities such as international cultural events, an International Symposium Series, and an annual Study Abroad Photo Contest.

Broadening Perspectives Through Global Opportunities

"At Webster, global citizenship is at the core of our mission; it is infused into the culture and curriculum across our worldwide network of campuses. Our nationally ranked study abroad program is a cornerstone of students' global learning experience."

~ *Assistant Director, Office of Study Abroad, Kimberly McGrath*

Webster University has one of the nation's most successful programs for undergraduates and graduates seeking to study internationally, due in large measure to the founding of the Office of Study Abroad (OSA) in 1994.

Webster's OSA coordinates a variety of international study opportunities on five continents for Webster students throughout the university's worldwide network of campuses. Programs range from single courses to degree programs requiring international study. OSA provides resources for students, parents, and faculty to make an international education a rewarding experience.

Assistance includes the Webster World Traveler program. Begun as the Freshmen Fly Free scholarship in 1995, the program provides free round-trip airline tickets to graduate and undergraduate students who qualify.

Hundreds of Webster's students use OSA's services to study abroad each year. Those services receive consistent high marks from ratings published by the Institute of International Education and *U.S. News and World Report.*

Chengdu Campus

1996 CHINA CAMPUSES

"This Webster University partnership marks the first time the Chinese government has approved an MBA program offered by an American university in China."

~ *President Richard S. Meyers*

By the dawn of the 1990s, Webster had established four thriving campuses in Europe, with London being the latest to open, in 1986. Richard Meyers brought a vision of further international expansion when he became president in 1994.

Meyers turned that vision into reality two years later by launching a campus in Shanghai, China, Webster's first venture in Asia.

The Shanghai campus filled an important need in a nation that desired the opportunity for its people to earn an MBA but whose institutions had the capacity to award only about 2,000 equivalent degrees annually. Webster University negotiated an arrangement with the Shanghai University of Finance and Economics, and the response was overwhelming: More than 1,300 applicants applied for the available fifty student openings. In short order, the Chinese Ministry of Education lifted a student cap and enrollment rose rapidly.

China's enthusiastic response to Webster's first venture in Asia led to additional Webster campuses in the country, expanding both undergraduate and graduate educational opportunities. Today, Webster has a partnership in Beijing with the Beijing Language and Cultural University, which also sponsors the university's Confucius Institute. And in Chengdu, Webster has developed a strong MBA program in partnership with the University of Electronic Science & Technology of China. These key partnerships have led to other collaborative programs in China such as a joint education studies and language program with Harbin University.

"We truly are an American institution in China, an NGO that is affecting Chinese and Americans alike," said Rick Foristel, Webster University China director.

Broadening Perspectives Through Global Opportunities

1999 THAILAND CAMPUS

Barely one year after Webster University opened its first Asian campus in Shanghai, China, it was already planning a second.

This one would be in Thailand.

Investors approached Webster about a campus in Cha-Am, ninety miles from Bangkok, and in July 1997 met with President Richard Meyers and Thai education officials. Negotiations went well, and before the end of the year, the Thailand Ministry of University Affairs approved the proposed Webster University campus.

The campus that opened in Cha-Am in 1999 offered quality educational programs and convenient access to cultural and recreational attractions. Though slowed by a struggling Thai economy in its early years, today the Cha-Am campus is a popular destination for students from Webster's other global campuses.

The capital city of Bangkok became home to a second Thailand Webster location which recently relocated to the heart of the business district in 2014. The Bangkok Academic Center provides undergraduate programs and graduate programs including business administration, international relations, and media communications.

Today more than 500 full-time students from sixty countries study at Webster's Thailand locations.

In 2013, Webster University Thailand was awarded the Thailand Trust Mark (TTM) by the Department of International Trade Promotion, Ministry of Commerce. The TTM was given to Webster Thailand in consideration of its academic quality, exceptional student diversity, recent international enrollment record, and customer service initiatives.

In the same year, Webster University Thailand was the only university to be awarded Thailand's prestigious Prime Minister's Business Enterprise Award, which recognizes exceptional Thai enterprises, particularly those that compete in the global marketplace. "I am delighted that our effort in promoting Thailand as an education destination and our quest for excellence has been recognized by the Thai Government," said Ratish Thakur, rector at Webster University Thailand.

Cha-Am Campus

Bangkok
Academic
Center

Broadening Perspectives Through Global Opportunities

Webster University's global emphasis added a new dimension in 2009 with the opening of the Confucius Institute.

Based at Webster's Old Post Office location in downtown St. Louis, the Confucius Institute promotes understanding of Chinese language and culture in cooperation with the Chinese Ministry

of Education and Webster's educational partner in Beijing, the Beijing Language and Cultural University (BLCU). There are 400 Confucius Institutes around the world, but Webster's was the first in Missouri.

Webster's Confucius Institute offers activities such as Chinese language instruction to elementary, high school, Webster, and adult education students. Other programs include Chinese cultural events at Webster University, summertime opportunities to study in China, faculty exchanges, and a visiting teachers program.

The Confucius Institute at Webster University achieved international recognition in 2012 and in 2014 when it was selected for the Confucius Institute of the Year award. "This award is a reflection of our continued commitment to international education, not only for our students, but for our community at large," said Dr. Deborah Pierce, director, Webster University Confucius Institute.

Confucius Institute
at Webster University

Neil George and Deborah Pierce at CI Opening

Mid-West Chinese Bridge Competition, 2013

President Stroble, Provost Schuster, BLCU President CUI Xiliand (seated) and Vice President QI Dexiang

合作协议签字仪

Signing Ceremony of Cooperation

崔希亮   戚德

2011 ACE INTERNATIONALIZATION LABORATORY AND DEANS' GLOBAL INITIATIVE

"The Internationalization Laboratory will provide the unique opportunity to share best practices with other institutions and to benefit from the expertise of the ACE senior staff."
~ President Beth Stroble and Provost Julian Schuster

National recognition of Webster University's reputation as a leader in global higher education came in 2011 with Webster's participation in the Internationalization Laboratory sponsored by the American Council on Education (ACE).

Together with seven other colleges and universities, Webster partnered with ACE's senior staff during 2011-12 "to create more globally engaged campuses with enhanced curricula and other international opportunities for their students," according to ACE.[13] Groups, or cohorts, of schools have been participating in the Internationalization Laboratories since 2003.[14]

Webster's work with the Internationalization Laboratory involved development of a strategic plan for long-term growth of Webster's global efforts.

Building on this important work is the Deans' Global Initiative, launched in 2013, which will ensure that every academic program offered by Webster includes a global component:

"We are truly poised for this moment and this opportunity to ensure each program has a significant global feature that only Webster can offer." – David Carl Wilson, dean of the College of Arts & Sciences

"We will do this in collaboration with our colleagues at Webster campuses throughout the world, as well as in professional and academic associations." – Brenda Fyfe, dean of the School of Education

"We are moving from a center-periphery model to a network model, from exporting American-style education, to making our US campuses a node in a worldwide network of global education." – Eric W. Rothenbuhler, dean of the School of Communications

"By that I mean we will do what no one else can do even if they wanted to. We will harness all our internal investments over the years to create a niche that makes Webster distinctive." – Benjamin Ola. Akande, dean of the George Herbert Walker School of Business & Technology

"To go forward, to pioneer, to innovate is not new for Webster. It's part of our history. It's part of our tradition." – Peter E. Sargent, dean of the Leigh Gerdine College of Fine Arts

2013 GHANA CAMPUS

"With this important location, we continue in the footsteps of our founders, who provided access to higher education in areas of greatest need, meeting students where they are."

~ *President Elizabeth (Beth) J. Stroble*

Teachers in Ghana often praise students who answer correctly by exhorting the class to "clap for them."

There was much clapping in Accra, the capital city of Ghana, when President Stroble and Provost Schuster established the university's first African campus there in 2013.

The campus offers opportunities for students to earn degrees recognized by Ghana and the United States. Webster successfully completed a rigorous process to earn accreditation from the Ghana Ministry of Higher Education and the United States Higher Learning Commission.

Webster chose Accra after careful study of potential sites throughout Africa. With a population of nearly 3 million, Accra is one of Africa's fastest-growing cities, a business and cultural center, and a transportation hub. Ghana is home to a rapidly growing economy based largely on energy, precious metals, and agriculture.

The Accra location offers courses in business, international relations, and communications, selected by Webster to reflect the interest of students and regional employers. Students in Accra also have the opportunity to take courses at other Webster campuses in Asia, North America, and Europe.

The Ghana campus links Webster University to its founders, the Sisters of Loretto, who have used education to minister to the poor in Ghana since the mid-1980s. The Sisters' work eventually led to the opening of a children's school with the Daughters of the Most Blessed Trinity near Kumasi, Ghana's second-largest city, in 2009.

Webster University's Accra campus greeted its first students in March 2014.

"Webster's presence in Ghana will be impactful and felt throughout the region," noted Provost Julian Schuster.

2014
ATHENS CAMPUS

Broadening Perspectives Through Global Opportunities

"In times of evolution and change, the organization of knowledge and experience sets the base for the new era. Progress is what lies ahead, with education acting as the means through opportunities fueled by our progressive mentality. This is what we all envision at Webster University Athens, in a transitional, but at the same time very promising period for us. Recent recognition of Webster University Athens by StudyAbroad101.com made all of us very proud. It was the best reward for our efforts to run world class study abroad programs."

~ Chancellor & Managing Director, Webster University Athens, Vasilis J. Botopoulos

Webster University's newest campus provides students with the opportunity to live and study in one of Western civilization's most significant locales, the city of Athens, Greece.

Acquired from the University of Indianapolis, the campus opened in the spring of 2015 as part of Webster's study abroad program. Students can enroll in a range of courses taught by Webster faculty over the course of an academic term, the summer, or the entire year. Future plans call for adding on-site undergraduate and graduate degree programs.

Students experience the latest—and the oldest—in Greek culture by living in furnished apartments near the campus located in the Plaka area in the center of Athens. Numerous restaurants, cafés, archaeological sites, and museums are within walking distance or a short ride away on local transportation.

"Greece is the birthplace of democracy, Western philosophy, Western literature, the Olympic games and much more and will be a great experience for students who wish to study abroad while also seeing the cradle of democracy firsthand," said Guillermo Rodriguez, director of study abroad and international projects.

2015 GLOBAL PARTNERSHIPS

"No other university offers so many ways to experience a global perspective and prepare students for the future."

~ *Provost, Senior Vice President and Chief Operating Officer Julian Z. Schuster*

In addition to an expansive network of global campuses, Webster partners with many other universities to create life-changing, global learning opportunities through a wide range of international programs—from faculty exchanges, field trips and summer classes to year-long programs and internships.

Webster students and faculty participate in unique projects, have valuable experiences, and build life-long relationships at these institutions, with more added each year:

Argentina: National University of Cuyo

Austria: Danube University Krems

Belgium: Haute École de Bruxelles

China: Beijing Language and Culture University; Harbin University; Shanghai University of Finance and Technology; Yunnan University of Finance and Economics

Cuba: University of Havana

Georgia: Caucasus University

Germany: Trier University

Hungary: St. Istvan; University of Pécs

Indonesia: President University

Italy: University of Modena and Reggio Emilia; Kent State-Florence

Japan: J. F. Oberlin University; Kansai University

Latvia: Daugavpils University

Mexico: Autonomous University of Guadalajara Sistema CETYS Universidad

Russia: South Ural State University

Slovakia: Bratislava Comenius University

Spain: University of Oviedo

Uzbekistan: Tashkent State University of Economics; Tashkent University of Information Technologies

Broadening Perspectives Through Global Opportunities

A DISTINCTIVE APPROACH TO THE EDUCATIONAL EXPERIENCE

From the beginning, Webster University has embraced change and growth not only among its students but among its faculty and staff as well. From support for continued faculty advancement and staff development to opportunities for students to achieve excellence in and outside of the classroom, the university has encouraged individuals to embrace their uniqueness. At the same time, Webster has fostered a sense of community through a variety of activities from early basketball games to contemporary group-based global citizenship projects. Today Webster University continues to explore new and innovative programs and reject the limitations of a "one size fits all" approach to education.

Cultivating Excellence in Teaching, Learning, and Scholarship   78

Unconventional Paths to Quality Learning Experiences   90

Student-Centered Learning in the Disciplines   102

Growing School Spirit   204

Enriching Learning through Community Partnerships   218

"The conference's ultimate purpose . . . is the educational unification of its members [and] immediate adoption of methods and aids to better teaching."

~ *President George F. Donovan, 1936*[15]

The tradition of cultivating excellence in teaching, learning, and scholarship at Webster University reaches back to the school's earliest days

In an era of severely limited opportunities for women in higher education, many Sisters of Loretto on the faculty at Loretto College had studied at Catholic University in Washington, DC. Sr. Mary Borgia Clarke, head of Loretto College's mathematics department, was the first student to enroll in advanced mathematics courses at St. Louis University.

Similar encouragement of faculty scholarship continued after Loretto College became Webster College. In the late 1920s, French instructor Marcelle Prévost spent a year aboard, and Clarke was given leave from teaching to study for a doctorate in philosophy in 1932.

Starting in 1933, the Sisters of Loretto launched an educational conference for all its members who were teachers, including the faculty at Webster. Held almost every year into the 1960s, the conference provided an environment for discussion, an opportunity to share best practices, and a chance to learn from distinguished speakers.

Webster College faculty and administrators presented at several of the conferences. President George Donovan shared papers on the organization of college curricula and student contact programs. Sr. Mary Mangan and Sr. Ann Patrick Ware examined contemporary movements and their impact on education. These faculty and administrators, like current Webster faculty and administrators, valued the opportunities to share their knowledge and experience with others and to learn from their colleagues and their students.

1970 FACULTY DEVELOPMENT LEAVE

The transition to a secular institution in 1967 forced Webster's administrators and faculty to face many issues, including tenure, which had never before been offered at Webster.

A number of tenure proposals were discussed, including one presented in January 1969. The plan was designed to closely follow the tenure guidelines established by the American Association of University Professors.

Dr. Leigh Gerdine, who became president in 1970, was not ready to rush into a traditional tenure program, stating: "The fact that Webster does not have a policy on tenure seems to me to be a great opportunity that has to be thought through very carefully, with the college's long range best interests in view, and not the immediate interests of myself or any other individual." As a result, "the faculty was encouraged to explore other programs that might be of greater benefit to the young, mobile faculty members."

In February 1970, the Faculty Constituent Assembly passed what was known as the short-term sabbatical program, which offered short-term sabbaticals after three, four, or five years of non-interrupted contracts at Webster. Approval by the Board of Trustees came the following December.

Today the short-term sabbatical program is known as faculty development leave (FDL), one of the oldest tenure alternative programs in the United States.[16] Although traditional tenure is also available, in 2015 over half of the eligible faculty at Webster were on the FDL track.

1977 MESSING AND KEMPER AWARDS

Since 1977, the Wilma and Roswell Messing Jr. Faculty Award has provided a stipend to a full-time faculty member for summer activity that strengthens teaching and learning at Webster. Faculty proposals are peer-reviewed by an appointed university committee.

The first recipient of the Messing Award was Dr. Neil George, former Webster vice president and chancellor, who at the time was chair of the History and Political Science Department. He used the funds to set up a student internship program to study the operations of Missouri state government.

The Kemper Award for Excellence in Teaching provides monetary awards for up to two full-time and two part-time instructors each year who demonstrate teaching at its finest. The award has been funded by a grant from the William T. Kemper Foundation of Commerce Bank since 1991.

Both awards exemplify Webster's strong commitment to exceptional teaching and learning, a tradition begun by the Sisters of Loretto which continues today.

Since 2013, the Kemper Foundation has generously funded the annual William T. Kemper Speaker on Excellence in Teaching & Learning. Kemper speakers are brought to campus to encourage and cultivate great teaching and learning through faculty workshops and a keynote speech.

2013 Kemper Award Winners Celebration featuring L-R, Kristen DiFate, Leon Hutton, Julie Palmer, Seth Leadbeater, President Stroble, Provost Schuster, and Jenny Hoelzer

1979 WEBSTER FILM SERIES

"Nowhere else in town will you see the idea of cinema as a unique and vital art form celebrated the way it's celebrated here, which is to say, continuously, joyously and often."

~ The Riverfront Times[17]

A cinema aficionado stepping back into the 1970s would find no readily available films, popular or otherwise, save for the latest Hollywood fare at theaters. DVDs, streaming video, and 24-7 movie channels lay years in the future.

One of the few alternatives for the St. Louis movie-going public was the Webster Film Series. Growing out of a student club called the Webster Film Society, which screened weekly movies, the official Webster Film Series launched in 1979.

It thrives today, just as it did in its early years, by screening a wildly eclectic range of cinema. Student films, foreign flicks, serious documentaries, classic movies—these and more make up the far-from-typical offerings of the Webster Film Series.[18] The series also features guest speakers who range from animators to actors to directors to musicians.

From its beginning, the Webster Film Series has been a staple of the St. Louis community and has been recognized locally and nationally.

In honor of the university's Centennial, the Webster University Film Series featured *A Century Through Cinema,* which highlighted 100 years of cinema with award-winning films that captured decades, defined generations, and evoked nostalgia.

1983 NAME CHANGE TO WEBSTER UNIVERSITY

"Formally operating as a university clearly announces to the public a structure that we have had for a decade."

~ *Board Chairman Robert C. West*

By the early 1980s, Webster had long ceased to be a small local Catholic college for women.

The college had expanded to remote sites in St. Louis and numerous locations around the nation, and, beginning in 1978, had opened campuses in Europe. In addition, the curriculum had increased in breadth and depth, including the addition of master's programs, and there were plans to develop the university's first doctoral degree.

The word "college" no longer seemed appropriate.

"Because of its growth and development, Webster as an institution defies easy classification," vice president and dean of faculty Dr. Joseph P. Kelly said in 1983. "We struggled for some time to find the right word to describe our history of educational innovation. 'University' fits better than any other designation because it implies the importance of academic traditions while suggesting a breadth of activities consistent with Webster's mission."

The decision to become Webster University took effect on February 1, 1983.

Sr. Mary Mangan

Sr. Mary Mangan, former Webster student and beloved faculty member, brought the Great Decisions program to Webster alumni in the 1990s. This program is the Foreign Policy Association's public education initiative to create more informed and engaged citizens by bringing people together to discuss US foreign policy and global affairs issues. The Webster University Alumni Association sponsors one of many Great Decisions groups throughout the nation.

Each year, the Foreign Policy Association selects several global topics and provides teacher guides with information on each topic. The Alumni Association partners with Webster's Department of History, Politics & International Relations to recruit Webster faculty and guests to serve as speakers for each topic. Webster's Center for International Education provides additional support for the program.

Webster's Great Decisions discussion group has grown from a dozen or so attendees to as many as 100 alumni and guests. In 2010, Webster received an honorable mention from the Foreign Policy Association, which recognizes the achievements of individual groups nationally.

Today, Webster professor and former Missouri governor Bob Holden holds a complementary Pizza & Politics series that introduces students, faculty, staff, and members of the community to influential public policy makers.

Robin Carnahan and Bob Holden

Cultivating Excellence in Teaching, Learning and Scholarship

Cultivating Excellence in Teaching, Learning and Scholarship

"The library of the 21st century is active, social, contextual, and engaging. Emerson Library is all this and more, with rich and varied resources, professional and energetic staff, and student/faculty/ community-owned environments that promote research, scholarship, and deep learning."

~ *Dean of University Libraries Laura O. Rein*

The 71,500 square-foot Emerson Library opened in 2003 as the intellectual center of Webster's global network. Designed by noted architectural firm Perry Dean Rogers and located in the heart of the home campus, Emerson Library provides engaging and student-owned environments with wired reading and study spaces, reference and access services, collaborative study rooms, and media facilities. A spacious conference room, Faculty Development Center, classroom, displays, and art installations further enhance Emerson Library's role as a central teaching and learning destination.

The neighboring outdoor quad developed along with the library serves as a meeting place and site for outdoor student events.

The library pioneered a comprehensive approach to providing the same level of services and resources to all Webster students, faculty, and staff worldwide, regardless of location. All library services, as well as rich digital and print library research materials, are available through the library's robust web site.

As an active partner in the academic mission of the university, the library is committed to finding innovative and creative ways to meet the teaching, learning, and scholarship needs of students, faculty, and staff.

2003 FACULTY DEVELOPMENT CENTER

"We're not only serving others more effectively the more effective we become as teachers, but we serve ourselves and grow ourselves professionally."

~ President Elizabeth (Beth) J. Stroble

Since 2003, the Faculty Development Center (FDC) has supported and promoted the achievement of excellence in teaching, learning, and scholarship of Webster's worldwide community of faculty. The FDC also provides instructional development, design, assessment, and technology consultation to maximize teaching effectiveness and student learning.

In the FDC, faculty members can work privately or with FDC staff, meet with their peers, attend events and workshops, and participate in learning communities. The center makes the same opportunities available virtually to faculty at all Webster University locations.

An advisory council of faculty members promotes the center, assists the center's staff in strengthening existing and developing new initiatives, and measures the center's effectiveness. The center's faculty fellows, selected from among the full-time faculty,

support fellow instructors through workshops, regularly scheduled meetings and individual consultations.

The center also holds an annual Teaching Festival in partnership with the Online Learning Center and the Emerson Library. Each year since 2011, the festival has shared best teaching practices through individual presentations, poster sessions, and panel discussions.

2007 WEBSTER UNIVERSITY PRESS

Cultivating Excellence in Teaching, Learning and Scholarship

"The decision to open a university press in an era when many were closing represented the firm commitment of a forward-looking administration to disseminate scholarly works that support the university's academic mission."

~ Dean of University Libraries and Editor of Webster University Press Laura O. Rein

Small-farm growers, Missouri environmental issues, a farewell to Kodachrome . . . these are book-length topics that might not have made it to print were it not for the Webster University Press.

Begun in 2007, the Webster University Press (WUP) supports Webster's mission with publications relevant to Webster's academic programs. WUP works with co-publisher Reedy Press to produce, market, sell, and distribute publications. WUP's editorial board accepts formal book proposals from Webster faculty and other members of the Webster community, as well as authors not connected with Webster. The board partners with outside peer-reviewers to reach decisions on proposals.

Encountering Florence, which explores Florence, Italy, through photos by Webster University professor Susan Hacker Stang, marked WUP's first publishing effort. One of its best-selling books has been *Massoud: An Intimate Portrait of*

the Legendary Afghan Leader, written by Webster alumna Marcela Grad. *Kodachrome: End of the Run* featured a Webster faculty/student project marking a key moment in photographic history. WUP has published seven books, including *Webster University: A Century of Defining Moments.*

2011 TEACHING FESTIVAL

"This Teaching Festival will bring . . . together people with new ideas, and thus improve something we do best — and that is to be excellent teachers."

~ *Provost, Senior Vice President and Chief Operating Officer Julian Z. Schuster*

Webster University has taken the idea of sharing best practices to a higher, all-inclusive level through its annual Teaching Festival, which is sponsored by the Faculty Development Center in partnership with the Emerson Library and the Online Learning Center.

Originating from discussions at a Faculty Fall Institute, the Teaching Festival was established in 2011. Held annually over several days each year, it features leading faculty members throughout Webster's worldwide network who share excellent practices they have developed during years of experience in traditional and online instruction. One of the highlights of each festival is a panel discussion of teachers who have won Kemper Awards, given each year to instructors who demonstrate teaching at its finest. In addition, a poster session allows faculty to interact with attendees and answer questions about instructional initiatives and projects.

Technology enables faculty at all of Webster's campuses to participate in real time as presenters or as audience members. Festival presentations are stored online, creating a growing archive of excellent ideas available to all faculty members at any time.

2014 Kemper Awards Winners Panel Discussion

Flora Lauten, Gad Guterman, and Raquel Carrio

Looking back at her time as a college student, President Beth Stroble recalled that "some of the worlds that were opened for us, the notions that we began to entertain that we had not been aware of, had come so many times from interacting with people outside of the university community."[19]

With that in mind, President Stroble launched two speaker series in 2012 to deliver thought-provoking ideas to students, faculty, staff, alumni, and the community: Contemporary Conversations for a Connected World and Global Leaders in Residence.

Contemporary Conversations for a Connected World provides lectures from progressive, bold, provocative leaders. Speakers in the series have included United Nations ambassador and civil rights leader Andrew Young, Emmy award-winner Bob Dotson, and OECD Ambassador Constance A. Morella, among many others.

Guest lecturers in the Global Leaders in Residence series visit the home campus for several days or weeks and interact with students and faculty in addition to formally addressing larger audiences. Global Leaders have included educator and author Jonathan Kozol, economist and educator Richard D. Wolff, World Wide Fund for Nature president Yolanda Kakabadse, award-winning filmmaker Steve James, dramatist and philanthropic leader Ben Cameron, and the co-founders of Cuban theatre company Teatro Buendia, Flora Lauten and Raquel Carrio.

Both series build on a Webster University tradition that reaches back to the early days of the college when distinguished guest speakers delivered lectures or spoke at commencement ceremonies. Key US government leaders, including President George H.W. Bush, have spoken at Webster, as have notable individuals who have shaped history, including Cesar Chavez, Henry Kissinger, Dr. Elizabeth Kübler Ross and Elie Wiesel, among many others.

PROVOST'S STUDENT/FACULTY COLLABORATIVE RESEARCH GRANTS

Webster University undergraduate psychology majors Sara McMullin, Ian Simpson, and Kayla Theberge spent much time and effort researching issues in their field of study. Their findings normally would have remained unknown to anyone outside a small circle of peers and instructors.

But the university's Provost's Student/Faculty Collaborative Research Grants, a program established by Provost Julian Schuster in 2014, enabled the three students to present their research to a wider audience at the annual conference of the Midwest Psychological Association.

The priceless experience made possible for McMullin, Simpson, and Theberge, and five other undergraduate students given grants to help with their research, perfectly illustrates the intent of the program. Undergraduate students conducting research under guidance of a faculty member can apply for funds to enhance research efforts. In addition to presenting findings at conferences, some of the other grant recipients published their research in peer-reviewed journals.

"The Provost's Student/Faculty Collaborative Grant program represents a significant step for Webster University," said associate professor of psychology Dr. Eric A. Goedereis. "I appreciate that the definition of 'research' is broad enough so that students and faculty from a variety of disciplines may take advantage of this opportunity by collaboratively exploring a topic of interest in a formalized way that is both professional and meaningful to the larger field. As important is the fact that the program emphasizes and supports the 'student-initiated' aspect of the work, which is consistent with Webster's mission to provide high-quality learning experiences and promote individual excellence."

Cultivating Excellence in Teaching, Learning and Scholarship

1965 WEBSTER ELIMINATES GENERAL DEGREE REQUIREMENTS

"If an undergraduate program suggests that there is some 'minimum requirement' of courses which guarantees that one is liberally educated, it gives us the right to abdicate interest in other areas by excluding them from the minimum requirement."

~ *Sr. Jacqueline Grennan,*
  then Executive Vice President

The year was 1964. Change seemed everywhere. The Beatles-led British invasion had conquered America. Lyndon Johnson overwhelmingly retained the presidency in November's elections. The Second Vatican Council was bringing the Catholic Church into the modern world.

In a decade when questioning convention had become standard thinking, Sr. Jacqueline Grennan and many of her peers at Webster began to question the need for requiring specific courses over a broad range of subjects. Better to let students choose their paths, rather than forcing them to acquire a shallow general knowledge of many subjects, some educators suggested.

The issue pitted academic freedom against rigid curricula. This was an especially thorny dilemma at Webster, at the time a Catholic college that required all students to take theology courses. Despite her religious affiliation, Grennan opposed all required general courses, even those in theology. Most of Webster's faculty supported her view, and in early 1965, they voted to eliminate general course requirements. Such requirements would remain eliminated for nearly thirty years, until 1992.

General education was reimagined most recently in 2011 with the Global Citizenship Program, but today the university still supports and promotes highly individualized educational paths for its diverse mix of students.

1965 STUDENT SABBATICALS

Amidst a decade marked by constant change, Webster chose to offer students a learning opportunity different from the traditional classroom model: the sabbatical. Similar to programs available to faculty, the sabbatical option allowed students to take a semester off from classes to work on a project under the direction of a faculty supervisor. Students could earn up to fifteen credit hours for the semester.

In the beginning, enrollment was limited to juniors and seniors in the behavioral and social sciences. Projects included teaching in an inner-city preschool, working at a mental hospital, and assisting in speech therapy and remedial reading activities.[20] Later, students in other disciplines did everything from work on political campaigns to study British and European theatre.

In addition to the off-campus sabbatical option, an experimental on-campus option was implemented in spring 1970. This latter program put more emphasis on student responsibility for learning, asking students to create their own learning objectives and evaluate their own projects.

An interesting variety of experiences grew out of both programs. Two students opened and operated a coffeehouse on campus. Another student worked on productions for KETC Channel 9, the local public television station. Other projects included teaching art at a mental hospital, teaching guitar to students at Webster's College School, and working with a local non-profit organization to train people with intellectual disabilities for industrial jobs.[21]

1966

NEWSWEEK RECOGNIZES WEBSTER UNIVERSITY AS ONE OF THE SCHOOLS LEADING A REVOLUTION IN TEACHING

"At Webster College, in St. Louis, Mo., elementary-science teachers learned this summer how to teach the discovery method by using the ultimate in cheap equipment: the common housefly."
~ Newsweek, 1966[22]

Unconventional Paths to Quality Learning Experiences

Webster College gained the attention of *Newsweek* in 1966 for highly effective teacher education. As part of a longer essay in its September 26, 1966, issue on new ways of teaching, *Newsweek* singled out Webster's master of arts in teaching program. The magazine described how elementary teachers in Webster's program learned ways in which common houseflies could serve as teaching tools that were every bit as effective as expensive lab equipment.

The segment on Webster concluded—"The point:

children can learn—often with the simplest tools —by themselves at their own speed if teachers use imagination."[23]

Today, the School of Education continues this tradition through such programs as those provided through the Beatrice and David Kornblum Institute for Teaching Excellence, which supports innovative education, program development, community service, and improved teaching and learning with emphasis on disadvantaged urban children.

1973 EXPERIENTIAL LEARNING

Webster University, in cooperation with the Council of Adult and Experiential Learning, offers an opportunity for undergraduate students to earn credits for job experience that demonstrates college-level learning.

The practice of earning credits for experience at Webster University reaches back to 1973, when Webster launched the Contract Center on the St. Louis campus.

Webster created the Contract Center based on a proposal from faculty member Sr. Barbara Ann Barbato, who had learned of similar programs from a Danforth Foundation workshop. She requested a program that would oversee what were at the time separate Webster initiatives for credit by examination, independent study, student sabbaticals, and individualized majors.

The Contract Center provided a formal path for students to design projects or use experience that would qualify for college credit. Faculty members helped students write formal plans for faculty board approval. Approved plans, plus thirty hours of traditional courses, would earn degrees. For example, one Webster student earned credits for teaching drama part-time at several local schools.

President Leigh Gerdine called the Contract Center a "college without walls" that used "the entire community as an educational resource."

The Contract Center grew into today's individualized learning experiences program. The program responds to a wide variety of student requests for individualized learning options, such as independent study, internships, sabbaticals, integration of work experience with students' major programs of study, and credit by examination.

Sr. Barbara Ann Barbato

1973 WEBSTER ADMITTED INTO UNION FOR EXPERIMENTING COLLEGES AND UNIVERSITIES

The 1960s and early 1970s were periods of change, innovation, and experimentation at Webster. From the transition to a coeducational, secular college to the elimination of general degree requirements to the introduction of student sabbaticals, Webster proved open to new ideas in higher education.

Webster's innovative approach to teacher education in developing a master of arts in teaching program made Webster an acknowledged leader in the field. At the undergraduate level, progressive programs in mathematics and science education gained local and national recognition.

The desire to collaborate with other like-minded institutions led Webster to seek membership in the Union for Experimenting Colleges and Universities (UECU).

Formed in 1964, the UECU was a consortium of institutions committed to research and experimentation in higher education.[24] When it joined in 1973, Webster was one of just twenty-one schools that comprised the UECU.

Dean of the undergraduate college Dr. Charles Madden stated that in joining the UECU:

"We will be part of a consortium that is not only experimental, but has a mechanism for evaluation." He also anticipated that membership could help bring in grants as well as facilitate working with traditional accrediting agencies.

Webster has continued to build on its experiences with the UECU as it leads in innovation and academic excellence through initiatives such as online degree programs, hybrid courses, one-year MBA, global international relations program, and graduate online certificates, to name just a few.

Unconventional Paths to Quality Learning Experiences

"In addition to exposing our students to the stresses adolescents encounter while growing up, we wanted to help youth who could use what our students have to offer — knowledge, creativity and experience."

~ *Professor of Nursing Barbara Wehling, 1992*

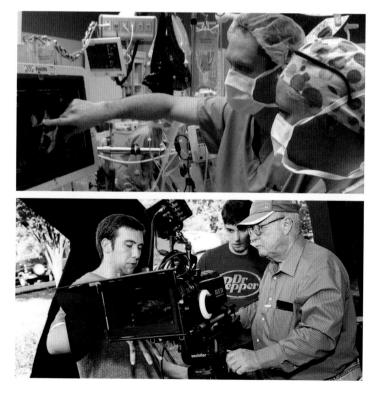

Throughout much of its history, Webster University has emphasized that students apply what they are learning to real-world situations. Initiatives such as The College School, an experimental teaching and learning lab founded in 1963, provided two important benefits: students learned by doing while helping the people they served.

Similarly, Webster launched three projects in the early 1990s that featured Webster students applying their knowledge to make a difference in the community.

The first, Student Literacy Corps, established in 1990, provided education majors teaching experience while helping low-literacy students in St. Louis schools, homeless shelters, and adult education centers. Get the Facts, established in 1992, saw Webster's nursing students working with teens at Mathews-Dickey Boys Club. In 1993, Webster launched ARCH—A Real Community Helps, a tutoring program in which Webster student volunteers helped children and parents improve reading skills.

Webster's focus on applied learning also can be seen in extensive internship opportunities in the United States and abroad. Two examples:

The Walker School of Business & Technology offers Walker EDGE internships around the globe, and the School of Communications helps about 150 undergraduates find internships annually. These and other internships at Webster provide invaluable career experience and make students stronger job candidates.

1998 ONLINE LEARNING

"Only online programs can facilitate the needs of a globalized workforce. I completed my studies while living in Princeton, Copenhagen, and Zurich. Who would have known that life would take me to three countries while working on my MA at Webster University?"

~ *Malene Cortelius (Class of 2013)*

In spring 1995, Webster University's Nursing Department connected the St. Louis and Kansas City campuses to teach a class by videoconference. From this modest beginning, Webster's massively popular global online learning initiative was born.

Webster's first Internet-based courses began as pilot programs in the School of Business & Technology and the School of Education in 1998. A year later, Webster's MBA and MAT programs went online, and other Webster degree programs followed soon after.

Online education opened another chapter in Webster's long history of taking higher education to non-traditional students. Anyone, anywhere, with a computer and an Internet connection, can take a class anytime. This is particularly significant for students who lack access to a traditional classroom. Says President Beth Stroble, "Webster started online programs in the 1990s, long before it was a fad. The first needs met were military service members deployed overseas; they wanted to keep moving on their degrees, but a face-to-face classroom wasn't even an option. So Webster began to develop according to student need."

Today, Webster offers more than twenty-five fully online graduate degree programs as well as undergraduate degree completion programs and both graduate and undergraduate certificates. Webster's global wide area network provides point-to-point videoconference technology to connect students and faculty throughout the worldwide network.

Webster's WorldClassRoom platform is created and maintained by the Online Learning Center at the home campus. The center's online learning experts work in partnership with the schools and colleges on Webster's online programs, which are recognized as some of the best in the nation by *U.S. News and World Report* and OnlineU.org.

"One of the things that's different about the Global Citizenship Program from the general education program . . . is that it's designed to have a beginning, middle and end, instead of a random cafeteria line of things you might sample."

~ Professor of Philosophy and Global Citizenship Program Director Bruce Umbaugh

Designed in 2011, the Global Citizenship Program (GCP) is a comprehensive array of undergraduate degree requirements that empowers students to thrive in a global future where jobs are created that do not exist today.

The program includes general education courses that address topics such as global issues, critical thinking, and written and oral communication. In addition, what helps make the GCP unique are beginning and keystone seminars.

First-year seminars acclimate students to Webster University and help them become better at integrating knowledge, thinking critically, and expressing themselves.

Keystone seminars, taken by juniors, comprise the GCP's final courses and address real-world projects. Each keystone seminar has an experiential component that actively involves students. One striking example is the global poverty learning simulation in the Real-World Survivor keystone, in which students experience third world poverty for four days at the Heifer Ranch Global Village. Webster students who participated in Real-World Survivor developed team solutions during the experience and presented their proposed solutions to audiences afterwards.

Unconventional Paths to Quality Learning Experiences

1915

RELIGIOUS STUDIES AND PHILOSOPHY

Student Centered Learning in the Disciplines: Arts & Sciences

It is no surprise that Webster, founded as a Catholic college, should have a strong tradition in religious studies and philosophy. In the early years, courses in these areas were taught almost exclusively by priests, especially faculty from Kenrick Seminary.

In addition to offering courses, in 1932 Webster began an impressive collection called the *Gallery of Living Catholic Authors* as a way to stimulate student interest in Catholic literature. Although the collection eventually moved to Georgetown University in 1980, for many years the Gallery reflected the focus on Catholic beliefs and spirituality that was Webster's heritage.

Sr. Ann Patrick Ware helped implement many changes to the theology curriculum, stating that "our aim is to make the courses relevant to the contemporary world in which the students live." In 1965, Ware hosted a television show called "The Word, Scripture and Man," where she discussed religious issues with noted Protestant theologian and Eden Theological Seminary faculty member Dr. Walter Brueggemann.

As Webster transitioned from a Catholic college

to a secular one, the openness to exploring other faith systems and cultures remained. Dr. Dennis Klass, former chair of the religion department who taught at Webster for over twenty-five years, noted that by the 1990s, the department had moved "from a primarily western theological department to a department that now shares all of the religions of the world." Today's Department of Religious Studies offers majors and a minor in many aspects of religious systems, as well as a certificate in Buddhist Studies.

Similarly, faculty in the Department of Philosophy teach and research in a wide variety of areas. The department is particularly noted for its role in promoting the study of international human rights. Art Sandler, former chair of Webster's Department of Philosophy, provided passionate leadership in this area and was instrumental in getting human rights added to the curriculum.

As part of its mission, the Department of Philosophy also administers Webster's Center for Ethics, which promotes discussion of various ethical positions within the university and the larger community.

Buddhist Sand Mandala

Art Sandler

DO NOT TOUCH ...!

Dennis Klass with graduates

Sr. Ann Patrick Ware
on "The Word,
Scripture and Man"

Lorettine

VOLUME XIII   NUMBER 3

Webster University's emphasis on original literature is almost as old as the school itself.

Beginning in November 1916, a year after the school started, enthusiasts of creative writing could get their fill from the *Lorettine*. An annual subscription of $1 bought four issues of short stories and poems by students and alumni, keynote addresses from faculty and guest speakers, and news of the school.

Contributors included Elizabeth Christman, class of 1935, who became a novelist and a respected professor of writing at the University of Notre Dame. Popular issues included the January 1941 *Lorettine*, devoted entirely to Webster's 25th anniversary.

Although the *Lorettine* ceased in the late 1960s, the publication is remembered as an important outlet for budding and established creative writers.

The students who contributed to the *Lorettine* were no doubt encouraged by the inspirational faculty who have taught in the English Department through the years, including Sr. Deborah Pearson, Dr. Reta Madsen, and Dr. Harry James Cargas. Besides the *Lorettine*, students were active in organizations such as the Poetry and Short Story Clubs.

The lofty standard set by the *Lorettine* continues with the English Department's creative writing program. Begun in 1986, the program focuses "on learning the art of reading as a writer: opening up influences, gathering strategies, widening the range of what's possible in a student's own writing."

The program exposes students to the best in current and past writing, using that knowledge to inspire students' own creative writing.

Harry James Cargas

Reta Madsen and Sr. Deborah Pearson with students

LITERATURE AND WRITING

Today, creative student writers have outlets for their work in two publications, *The Green Fuse* and *The Webster Mercury*. The yearly *Green Fuse* and its predecessor, the *Writer's Circle Magazine*, have been publishing the best in poetry, fiction, drama, translations, and nonfiction from Webster students worldwide since the early 1980s. The English Department has been publishing exceptional work written for its courses in *The Webster Mercury* and its predecessor, *The Right Reader*, since 1973.

Creative writing students hear from the nation's top authors, playwrights, and poets in the English Department's Visiting Writer Series, a staple at the home campus since 1986.

Most importantly, Webster's creative student writers learn from faculty members who are working creative writers themselves. Creative writing at Webster University typifies the College of Arts & Sciences' "belief in free and rigorous intellectual inquiry. . . that. . . comes alive in our classrooms every day thanks to our distinctive faculty and diverse body of students."

The faculty of the creative writing program includes award-winning playwright Michael Erickson, literary critic Dr. Margot Sempreora, and Webster alumnus Murray Farish, whose first book of short stories appeared on the list of Best Books of 2014 compiled by the *St. Louis Post-Dispatch.*

David Clewell, director of the English Department's creative writing program states: "The program has many strengths. It's a small program with a lot of individual attention for students. But the strongest aspect is, lucky for us, the professors of creative writing are also full-time, published writers in their respective genres."

Clewell himself has authored eight collections of poetry, and his work has won two national awards. In 2010, he was named Poet Laureate of Missouri by Governor Jay Nixon, who noted: "You don't have to spend very long with David Clewell, or his poetry, to know that he has a unique perspective on contemporary American life and the characters and ideas that loom large in our recent history."

David Clewell

Student Centered Learning in the Disciplines: Arts & Sciences

The dawning of the 1930s convinced some forward-thinking Americans that isolationism was impossible. The global Depression and the rise of communism, fascism, National Socialism, and militarism demonstrated that the United States was not immune from the impact of events elsewhere.

One of those forward-thinking Americans became Webster College's president in 1931. Dr. George Donovan, the school's first lay president, inspired a global perspective in Webster's students that remains a hallmark of Webster University and the College of Arts & Sciences today.

One of Donovan's first actions was to begin a mandatory course in current events, which he taught. *The New York Times* became required reading for freshmen.

Donovan's early tenure as president included the founding of a student International Relations Club, which would continue at Webster until at least 1963. Such clubs were founded at a number of US colleges under the sponsorship of the Carnegie Endowment for International Peace, and fostered activities such as model assemblies of the League of Nations, the forerunner of

the United Nations. Webster became the first Catholic women's college to hold a model assembly in March 1934.

Webster's interest in the United Nations led the college to host the President's Commission for the Observance of the 25th anniversary of the United Nations on October 20, 1970. Webster College was one of only four locations in the country for the hearings chaired by Senator William Fulbright of Arkansas.

The College of Arts & Sciences has continued the international traditions begun by Donovan.

One of the best examples of this enduring global outlook is the global master of arts in international relations (GMAIR) begun in 2006. Students study at five international locations during the program and cover topics such as war and diplomacy, international law, US foreign policy, globalization and human rights.

Says one GMAIR student, Ann Nguyen: "Being able to travel and expose myself to so many new cultures; visiting numerous international organizations such as Organization of the Petroleum Exporting Countries, the United

Nations, and the Vienna Center for Disarmament and Non-Proliferation; and just learning how to be a well-rounded global citizen have all been extraordinary experiences. I've been able to learn so many things both about myself and the world around me that I never would have been able to discover without this program."

Kristen Morton

Alice Cochran

Fulbright Hearings

HISTORY, POLITICAL SCIENCE, INTERNATIONAL RELATIONS, AND LEGAL STUDIES

In addition to the global master of arts in international relations, the Department of History, Politics and International Relations (HPIR) offers a certificate in migration and refugee studies at the Geneva campus, the home of the annual International Humanitarian Conference.

The College of Arts & Sciences provides another memorable global educational experience with its courses in Leiden, the Netherlands, sponsored by the Department of Legal Studies. Students can take advantage of the Leiden campus's proximity to The Hague to visit such key institutions as the International Criminal Court.

The many innovative programs in history, political science, international relations, and legal studies have been made possible through the years not only through supportive administrators but by committed faculty who took a broad and interdisciplinary view of their disciplines. Dr. Conal Furay, who joined Webster in 1966, developed courses on nontraditional topics such as the history of business and management, and Dr. Alice Cochran, who taught for almost forty years at Webster, stressed to her students the interconnectedness of history with art, literature, and culture. Sr. Mary Mangan had a background in minority studies but was equally known for her international relations and current events courses. Dr. Julia Walsh was an expert on the American South and slavery and an important contributor to the women's studies program as well.

Complementing the HPIR Department's programs are those of the Institute for Human Rights and Humanitarian Studies. For example, faculty and students from across Webster's network utilize the institute's resources to study the evolving worldwide crisis of human trafficking. Webster's Leiden campus has undertaken sustained direct action to help ameliorate the impact of trafficking in the Netherlands through the Bijlmer project. Created in 2012, the project combines academic research and community intervention to promote awareness of the issue and help ensure that the social and psychological needs of victims are met. Classes on the issue of human trafficking are taught at Webster campuses in St. Louis, Thailand, and Leiden. Through the institute, students and faculty are able to collaborate with one another and benefit from research and connections that take learning outside of the classroom.

Global MAIR cohort in Leiden

Conal Furay

Sr. Mary Mangan

Burcu Pinar Alakoc

1944

Student Centered Learning in the Disciplines: Arts & Sciences

Today's social and behavioral sciences and counseling programs in the College of Arts & Sciences can trace their roots back to the very early years of the college.

In 1916, Rev. Joseph P. Donovan, a professor at nearby Kenrick Seminary, joined the college and taught courses in ethics and social sciences for many years. Psychology was usually included in the form of a course or two in the philosophy program.

Webster established an undergraduate sociology major in 1944. In 1963, a rising interest in related areas led to sociology moving into a new Social Science Department along with anthropology, psychology, economics, political science, and geography.

The Social Science Department of the 1960s emphasized a practical, experiential approach. Students could undertake in-depth studies in hospitals and agencies through a sabbatical program and conduct research in various laboratories on campus.

Through the years, students have had the benefit of learning from faculty who have taken an

active role in the community. Sr. Felicia Corrigan, former chair of the Sociology Department in the 1950s and early 1960s, was an advisor to the Interracial Justice Commission at Webster. Sr. Ann Christopher Delich lived and worked at the Webster-Mullanphy Center in the inner city while teaching at the college. Faculty in anthropology, sociology, psychology, and related disciplines have inspired others through their teaching, research, and service and have encouraged their students to do the same.

It's no wonder then that interest in these disciplines continued to grow. Psychology appeared as a separate major in the 1975/76 course catalog. After many years as a combined Behavioral and Social Sciences Department, two new departments were formed in 2014: Psychology and Anthropology/Sociology.

The faculty in these departments have also expanded the offerings available to their students. In Psychology, there is a new emphasis area in mental health and an option to earn a B.S. in psychology with additional coursework in human biology and genetics. In Anthropology & Sociology, students can major in cultural anthropology and sociology, women and gender studies and criminology.

Counseling joined Webster's social sciences offerings in 1975 and became a separate Department of Professional Counseling in 2013. Dr. William HuddlestonBerry, who led the program for many years, summed up the continuing need for qualified counseling professionals with Webster's global focus: "It really is a global issue. Peoples of the world are constantly confronted with cultural and interpersonal conflict: natural disasters; disease and famine; war and genocide; discrimination and oppression. And the job of the mental health counselor must attend to all of these global phenomena."

William HuddlestonBerry

BASS Research Club

Sr. Ann Christopher Delich

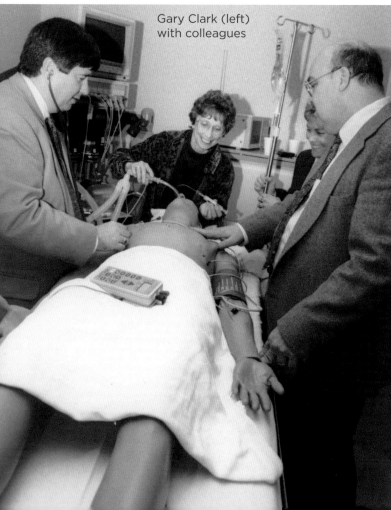

Gary Clark (left) with colleagues

1980 NURSING/NURSE ANESTHESIA

Unlike other disciplines, nursing is a relatively recent addition to the Webster curriculum. Webster University's nursing program started in Kansas City, MO, in 1980 through an agreement with St. Luke's Hospital School of Nursing in that city. A few years later, a similar program was initiated in St. Louis through a partnership with St. Luke's Hospital.

From the beginning, Webster's nursing program has focused on the needs of the working professional nurse. As Dr. Dian Davitt, associate professor of nursing, explained: "Our BSN program is different than most in that we focus on the adult learner. Our students are often balancing full-time jobs, families, and school. We offer them flexibility and an individualized program."

Another option for the adult student is a combined BSN/MSN degree, which Webster began offering in 1993. In addition, that same year Webster responded to the growing focus on the family by starting an MSN in family-centered health care. According to Dr. Janice Hooper, chair of the nursing department at the time, "With the changes in the health care arena, more families are becoming involving in caring for family members with health problems at home . . . we felt that offering a master's degree in family nursing was appropriate." Webster's nursing programs and degrees are accredited by the Accreditation Commission for Education in Nursing.

Another successful health-related program was added in 1997 when the master of science in nurse anesthesia program began under the leadership of Dr. Gary Clark. Four years later, a $772,000 federal grant funded expansion of the program into rural communities. According to Clark, the grant allowed Webster "to recruit students from rural and underserved areas and educate them so they can return to these areas and practice nurse anesthesia, filling a vital need."

Webster's nurse anesthesia program is unique in its emphasis on the sciences and the early exposure to clinical situations, where students integrate what they learn in the classroom into practical experience. The nurse anesthesia program is accredited by the Council on Accreditation of Nurse Anesthesia Educational Programs.

1995 COLLEGE OF ARTS & SCIENCES FOUNDED

With its focus on broad liberal arts and sciences education, the College of Arts & Sciences (CAS) offers the largest number of academic programs of Webster University's five colleges and schools.

As Webster grew to a university with 100 programs on campuses around the world in the 1980s, Dr. Neil George, then Webster's undergraduate dean, began reorganizing the university's many departments into a centralized structure, with CAS founded in 1995.

The first departments in CAS included History, Politics and Law; Foreign Languages; Behavioral and Social Sciences; Literature and Language; Philosophy; Religion; Nursing; and Science. Dr. William Eidson became the founding dean of CAS in 1996.

Dr. David Carl Wilson was appointed dean of the College of Arts & Sciences in 2002. During his tenure, he has witnessed the strong partnerships forged among the faculty, staff, and students in the college: "At many universities, faculty members are loyal to their disciplines . . . and not to their universities. At Webster it's the opposite," he said. "They are committed to the students and to working collaboratively with other faculty

and staff—they are very engaged, and so much creative thinking is going on. Our identity comes from being Webster people, and that's wonderful."

CAS has grown to encompass twelve departments that offer dozens of undergraduate, graduate, minor, and certificate programs that foster free and rigorous intellectual inquiry across a wide spectrum of subjects. In 2013, the college reorganized into two divisions—the Division of Liberal Arts & Humanities and the Division of Professional Programs.

CAS programs can be found at all of Webster's international campuses and at many US extended campuses, as well as online. In that global spirit, CAS also administers the Institute for Human Rights and Humanitarian Studies, which supports teaching, research, and service on human rights issues.

Webster's CAS undergraduate certificates reflect the college's diversity and global perspective, covering everything from international languages, to gender studies, international human rights, diversity and identity in the US, and ethics. Two certificates actually require all or part of the coursework to be completed at an international campus: migration & refugee studies, which is offered in Geneva, and Buddhist studies, which includes study at Webster's Hua Hin/Cha-am, Thailand campus.

Dean David Carl Wilson with students, 2014

Jane and Bruce Robert

Webster University helped kindle Jane Robert's love of all things French. In 1967, Robert (class of 1969) received a scholarship that "changed my life" to study at the Sorbonne during her junior year.

Robert went on to a career teaching French and promoting French culture. She has served at the highest levels in several national French-US cultural organizations and received numerous honors and awards. In 2010, Jane and her husband Bruce showed their appreciation for the university by endowing Webster's first faculty

professorship with a $1 million gift, one of the largest alumni gifts in Webster's history.

Dr. Lionel Cuillé, who specializes in 19th-21st century French literature, was named the inaugural Jane and Bruce Robert Professor in French and Francophone Studies. The Roberts' generosity also helped establish Le Centre Francophone, which sponsors programs about French culture.

Cuillé is the latest in a long line of distinguished faculty in the area of international languages and cultures. Dr. Jacques Chicoineau, who came to Webster in 1959, taught French at the university for twenty-five years. He served as faculty advisor to the Webster chapter of Pi Delta Phi, the French honor society, founded *La Jeanne d'Arc*, a student publication, and established an exchange program to send Webster students to France to teach for a year. He was known as a master puppeteer and was honored not only for his use of puppetry in his teaching but for his work in promoting the study of French and French culture.

Perhaps the language faculty member with the longest tenure in Webster's history is Consuelo

Gallagher. A native of Venezuela, Gallagher came to Webster in 1945 and taught for almost sixty years. She served for thirteen years as chair of the Modern Languages Department and was also a member of the first Faculty Steering Committee, established after the university's transition to a secular college in the late 1960s. In 2005, Gallagher received an Honorary Doctor of Laws degree from Webster, and in 2011, she was honored with the Daniel Webster Society Visionary Award.

These and many other faculty laid the groundwork for today's Department of International Languages and Cultures. The department offers instruction in eleven languages. Students can participate in exchanges with Argentina and France and internships in China, Germany, Mexico, and Japan. Students also have opportunities for short-term study abroad through hybrid courses.

Lionel Cuillé

Consuelo Gallagher

Jacques Chicoineau with students

Student Centered Learning in the Disciplines: Arts & Sciences

The biological and physical sciences have a long tradition at Webster University. Chemistry and biology were among the original sixteen courses taught at Loretto College when it opened in St. Louis in 1916, a year after operating at a temporary site in Kansas City. The east wing of the administration building, today's Webster Hall, included science labs equipped with the latest microscopes.

Several talented science faculty members have taught at Webster over the years. In the 1930s, Sr. M. Aloyse Ellington had her research published in *The Proceedings of the Society of Experimental Biology and Medicine*, marking the first time that a Catholic nun's work had appeared in that journal. Dr. William Walton earned recognition for his hands-on techniques that used simple materials to teach scientific concepts. Walton came to Webster in 1961 and taught physics, as well as playing an important role in Webster's nationally recognized master of arts in teaching program in the mid-1960s.

Virginia Harrison, a Webster graduate, inspired generations of students for twenty-five years. As chair of what was then the Science Department, she worked to build the program and improve the equipment and facilities available to the students.

Further indication of the vital role the sciences play at Webster will come in the near future with the construction of a new interdisciplinary sciences building, which will include a signature space named Browning Hall in honor of long-time supporters Laurance (Larry) and Jinny Browning. In 2015, the Brownings bestowed another significant gift of $1 million to establish the Laurance J. Browning Jr. Endowed Professorship in Biological Sciences. Larry Browning was a life trustee of Webster University and chairman of the Board of Trustees, and was associated with the board for twenty-six years.

Victoria Brown-Kennerly

Laurance and Jinny Browning

Virginia Harrison

1940 BUSINESS STUDIES

In the 1920s, Webster students who wanted to study business and management had to settle for secretarial courses which the college catalog claimed would "prepare those who wish to enter the field of business more readily to assume positions of leadership and responsibility." The program included courses in everything from shorthand and typewriting to accounting and commercial law.

President George Donovan saw a need to expand these offerings by starting a two-year business program in 1940. The new Department of Business Administration introduced courses in management styles and office procedures.

As Donovan explained: "Almost every college of liberal arts has compromised directly and indirectly in favor of professional subjects. Webster must recognize this tendency, and if it is to continue as a liberal arts college, it must meet this challenge."

During the 1943-44 school year, Webster began offering a B.S. in business administration. Courses listed in the 1946-47 catalog included a mix of secretarial courses and business courses such as personal finance, retailing and advertising, money and banking, and business law.

Although these early programs pale in comparison to the array of courses available in today's George Herbert Walker School of Business & Technology, they do reflect Webster's early commitment to educating women for leadership roles in a variety of careers.

President Donovan
with Elizabeth Halpin

1974 MANAGEMENT UNDERGRADUATE DEGREE PROGRAM

Dr. William Duggan was instrumental in the development of the individualized master of arts program to serve working adults in 1973. A year later he was back at the drawing board helping to put together another program to meet an unmet need, an undergraduate program in management.

Duggan received requests from the Army and Coast Guard for a degree completion program for their recruiters who had not finished undergraduate degrees and thus were ineligible for Webster's popular graduate programs for working adults. Duggan, who had led the development of the graduate programs, met the challenge by designing an undergraduate degree completion program in management. Webster offered the first few courses in the program in spring 1974, and official approval for the management B.A. was received that same year.

The program took shape that August with the hiring of Dr. Doris Beuttenmuller as director. Barely a week later, classes in group dynamics, mathematics for managers, human communications, and psychology of management began at several off-site locations in St. Louis.

Beuttenmuller formalized the program by hiring qualified faculty, developing an approved curriculum, and putting a student advising program in place. More off-site locations were added to meet increasing demand. In its first year, the undergraduate management program conferred degrees on thirty-three students. The second year saw the first on-campus classes, during the day and at night, in 1975-76, putting Webster on track toward today's George Herbert Walker School of Business & Technology.

Current students interested in a bachelor's degree in management have the option of focusing on an emphasis area such as health care administration, human resource management, international business, or marketing. They can also take advantage of global hybrid courses which combine online coursework with travel to locations around the world. Another unique opportunity was the recently offered management course, SPICE'ing UP Strategy, a seminar co-taught by grandmaster Susan Polgar, Webster University's chess head coach and founder of the Susan Polgar Institute for Chess Excellence.

Doris
Beuttenmuller

James
Brasfield

Student Centered Learning in the Disciplines: Business & Technology

2013 Doctoral Program Students

In the early 1970s, some Webster faculty and administrators were already thinking about creating the school's first doctoral degree. A few proposals were put together in the late 1970s, but it would be over a decade before the dream would become a reality.

Work began in earnest in 1983. Dr. Doris Beuttenmuller, director of the undergraduate management program, headed a committee of faculty and executive staff members that included Deans William Duggan and Neil George. Ten consultants provided input as the committee met frequently to plan for a doctorate program in business. The committee's work paid off when the Higher Learning Commission approved the request for change in status in the summer of 1987.

An unexpected problem confronted the university and its new doctorate in applied management (DAM) program. "Webster faculty and administrators were pleased to have the approval, but somewhat concerned about the DAM title," Beuttenmuller wrote dryly twelve years later. "They resolved to seek a change in title in the future."

Two years later, the program's name changed to its current title, doctor of management.

The first group of thirteen doctoral students began their classes in January 1988. From the start, the doctoral program focused on practitioners who wanted to take what they learned to the business world rather than teach at a university. The program drew students with a variety of backgrounds, from military personnel to nonprofit administrators. Today over thirty students are currently enrolled in the doctor of management program at Webster.

Mathematics and Computer Science, one of three departments in the George Herbert Walker School of Business & Technology, was formed in 1992. But its genesis can be found many years earlier.

Mathematics was offered as a major as early as the 1920s. Courses included geometry, trigonometry, algebra, calculus, differential equations, theoretical mechanics, and the history of mathematics. A "Teacher's Course" could also be taken which was "a critical review of algebra and geometry with a view to modern methods of teaching."

In the 1960s, Webster developed a national reputation for mathematics education through an innovative program called the Madison Project. The curriculum emphasized discovery and problem solving as opposed to "a knowledge of facts or memorized procedures." Dr. Robert Davis, the program director, along with faculty such as Katharine Kharas, led a movement to change the way mathematics is taught in elementary school.

Today students can apply their mathematics degree to a wide range of careers in addition to teaching. One of the most popular double majors at Webster is that of math and computer science.

It's fitting that computer science got its start at Webster thanks to a mathematician. Dr. Edward Sakurai, chair of the Mathematics Department, "had been doing research on the new 'personal computer' during his sabbatical back in 1977," wrote Anna Barbara Sakurai, his wife and fellow mathematics faculty member. "He was convinced that this development would revolutionize our lives."

Dr. Sakurai gained Webster's support to rent a Commodore Personal Electronic Transactor (PET) —one of the world's first personal computers— in spring 1977 and began a limited computer studies program on the St. Louis campus. A few rented Apple computers were added. The department bought its first computers—six PETs and four Apple II Plus models—in 1981-82. The Mathematics Department added Computer Studies to its title in 1984.

The first full-time computer science faculty members joined the department in 1991. A year later, the department changed its name to Mathematics and Computer Science (MCS), a title that remains today. MCS became part of the School of Business & Technology in 1995.

The early MCS adopted a philosophy in line with the vision of today's Walker School of Business & Technology that "enables real world success for students through an application-based curriculum and a supportive academic environment."

Anna Barbara Sakurai wrote about those days: "Our curriculum was technical at the same time as it was practical. Our goal was to prepare students for the future by teaching them the fundamentals of computer science, but we also wanted them to have enough practical training to be able to walk into a business and be immediately useful to their employers."

Carol Schwab

Edward Sakurai

John Aleshunas and Xiaoyuan Suo

1992 SCHOOL OF BUSINESS AND TECHNOLOGY FOUNDED

The 1980s witnessed tremendous growth at Webster University. More extended campuses were added, and enrollment doubled, reaching 9,675 in 1990.

Mindful of the pressures caused by rapid growth, undergraduate dean Dr. Neil George advocated for reorganizing Webster from many independent departments into schools and colleges. Meanwhile, Dr. Doris Beuttenmuller, who had directed Webster's undergraduate management program since 1974, successfully proposed a Department of Business and Management (DBM) in 1986.

Her long-range goal was the creation of a School of Business. That goal seemed logical, given that DBM offered more graduate programs with higher enrollments than any other department at Webster.

Much discussion followed, and several years passed. In 1992, Webster established the School of Business and Management, the first of what would become today's five schools and colleges that comprise Webster University. Incorporation of the Department of Mathematics and Computer Science in 1995 resulted in a name change to the School of Business & Technology. Dr. Wil Miles served as the founding dean of the school.

Of Webster's five schools and colleges, the School of Business & Technology serves the largest number of students, and its programs are included at all of Webster's extended campuses as well as online. In fact, the school offered one of Webster's first Internet-based courses. Begun as a pilot program in 1998, it consisted of five courses that linked students at the Geneva, Leiden, London, and Vienna campuses along with six US locations. A year later, Webster's MBA went fully online.

The school's business and management programs are accredited by the Accreditation Council for Business Schools and Programs. Dr. Benjamin Ola. Akande was appointed dean of the School of Business & Technology in 2000 and served until 2015. He described Webster's business school this way—"What we have is a school that has a diverse population of students and one common denominator: We are trying to transform their lives, make them aware of opportunities out there, and prepare them to be meaningful participants."

Dean Benjamin Ola. Akande with students, 2014

2001 WALKER SPEAKER SERIES

Industry luminaries, government leaders, best-selling authors, business educators . . . all have come to Webster University to participate in the Walker Speaker Series sponsored by the George Herbert Walker School of Business & Technology.

Started in 2001 by Dean Benjamin Akande, the series has brought more than 100 innovative leaders to share their business knowledge, management expertise, values, and career challenges with the Webster community.

In addition to a traditional address, the format sometimes includes a panel discussion among several participants from a particular field who entertain questions from the audience. The speeches and panels are archived on video and are accessible online by the public.

"When you look at the list of people we have brought here, you can see that nobody is too big for us," Akande said.

The speakers and their organizations are a who's who of industry, government, and education. General Motors, IBM, Oxford University, Twitter, and The Walt Disney Company are among those who have been represented in the Walker Series. Presidential advisers, senators, ambassadors, and a past chairman of the Joint Chiefs of Staff have offered their wisdom to Webster's audiences.

The Walker Series "is a great way for the school to reach out to the business community and to bring real-world experiences to an academic setting," former General Motors and AT&T chairman and chief executive officer Ed Whitacre said during his Walker Speaker Series address in 2005.

The series has given greater visibility to the George Herbert Walker School of Business & Technology and has brought important issues to audiences. But the most important reason for the series is simple, Akande said: "It's about our students. It's about giving them the exposure that enhances their capacity to be competitive in the marketplace."

Diane Sullivan

David Steward

Jack Dorsey

Dean Benjamin Akande with Maxine Clark

Student Centered Learning in the Disciplines: Business & Technology

George Herbert and Carol Walker

It would be difficult to find a stronger champion of the School of Business & Technology than the man for whom the school is named, Ambassador George Herbert Walker III.

The former US ambassador to Hungary, philanthropist, and St. Louis civic leader joined Webster's Board of Trustees in 1974. He was twice its chairman and was named life trustee in 2003. He served as chairman of the board of advisors to Webster's business school for many years. In honor of his support and achievements, the Board of Trustees established an endowed fund in his name, the Walker Leadership Award, given each year starting in 1997 to an outstanding graduating senior.

In 2007, Walker raised his support of Webster to an even higher level by giving $10 million to the School of Business & Technology, the largest single donation in Webster's history. At a special ceremony announcing the gift, Walker stated: "We are believers in the critical role of education in society. Education adds to the quality of life for all of us. It helps us understand where we come from and who we are." Webster University recognized Walker for his longtime service and support by naming the school the George Herbert Walker School of Business & Technology in his honor in 2010.

President Stroble and
George Herbert Walker III
and guests

![Webster UNIVERSITY]

Dean Benjamin
Akande with
George Herbert
Walker III

Ambassador Walker
and 2014 Walker
Leadership Award
Recipient Courtney
Turner

2014 CYBERSECURITY AND INNOVATION

Lynn Selders

"Webster University continues to be on the forefront of addressing the growing needs in our society and business community. Our uniquely designed cybersecurity program is another prime example of Webster's commitment to creating relevant and highly-impactful educational programs."

~ *Provost, Senior Vice President and Chief Operating Officer Julian Z. Schuster*

When the U.S. Air Force Space Command wanted to train its employees to defend their web-based systems from increasingly sophisticated hackers, the Air Force turned to Webster University for help. In response, the George Herbert Walker School of Business & Technology established a graduate degree program in cybersecurity in 2014.

The master of science in cybersecurity program prepares students to oversee, operate and protect critical computer systems, information, networks, infrastructures, and communications networks. "Cybersecurity is one of the fastest growing fields in the United States today, and we believe the demand for it will continue to grow as our society continues to become more interconnected online," said Dr. Thomas Johnson, associate vice president and chief of strategic initiatives, who helped develop the program. Graduates of the program will be able to propose solutions that secure networks from cyber attacks, which are increasing at alarming rates.

Cybersecurity is the latest in a number of programs that are carrying on a decades-old Webster University tradition of responding to the needs of its constituents. Another such program is the undergraduate degree in mobile computing, which was introduced in 2012. Individuals who can

create applications for mobile devices are in demand, according to Professor Martha Smith, who helped create the program.

Another area in need of qualified graduates is the growing field of forensic accounting. In 2011, the Walker School launched the MS in forensic accounting program which includes courses in criminal and civil investigation, legal procedure, management of evidence, cyber forensics, substantive law, valuation, economic damages, and internal auditing. Graduates of the program will have the ability to conduct successful investigations and be able to provide expertise in a variety of criminal and civil financial matters.

Webster is also meeting the needs of today's workforce through the creation of certificates for those individuals needing a short-term program in a specific area. The Walker School has developed certificates in entrepreneurship, global business, project management, and cybersecurity-threat stabilization and will no doubt be ready to respond with more innovative programs as needs arise in the future.

Debbie
Psihountas

Mary Bufe

2014

ONE-YEAR MBA

Webster University has met the educational needs of working adults throughout its history. One of the latest examples is the one-year master's in business administration program established by the George Herbert Walker School of Business & Technology.

With surveys showing significant growth in new MBA hires, the program is ideal for working adults who want to advance their careers through studying in a high-quality MBA program without long time commitments.

"This program recognizes that not everyone can afford long interruptions to their lives or career paths to obtain a graduate degree," said Dean Benjamin Akande. "The program does this without sacrificing quality, including practice and theory from various disciplines, and offering an integrated global curriculum that Webster is well known for weaving into all of its courses."

Offered at seven campuses around the world, the program provides instruction through a mix of in-person and online classes. Students progress through the program in a single group, or cohort, that takes each class together. The program commenced in fall 2014 on campuses in St. Louis, MO; Denver, CO; Kansas City, MO; Orlando, FL; Geneva, Switzerland; Leiden, the Netherlands; and Vienna, Austria.

The Walker School structured the program based partly on recommendations from a task force formed in 2013 to evaluate Webster's business programs.

The one-year MBA represents the latest in variations on Webster's MBA programs that serve working adults. These include an MBA-global track, a forty-two credit-hour program combining core MBA courses with internationally focused coursework. Students take twelve hours of approved international courses, including at least one three-credit one-week international trip.

Complementing the MBA-global track is a global business certificate program, which consists of twelve hours of internationally focused courses and a one-week international trip.

2014 WORLDWIDE CAREER MANAGEMENT AND COACHING PROGRAM

Studying for a graduate degree through Webster University's George Herbert Walker School of Business & Technology means establishing a relationship that lasts long after graduation, thanks to the career management and coaching program, launched in 2014.

The program starts while a graduate student is enrolled in the Walker School and continues past graduation, providing guidance throughout the student's career.

"Whether our students want to begin, advance, or change their careers, this new professional development program will equip them with the tools and resources they need to proactively manage their careers and achieve their goals," said Dean Benjamin Akande.

Offered in partnership with Right Management, the program provides a firm foundation in career management and includes individualized career coaching on key topics such as developing a career action plan, updating resumes, and strengthening interviewing and negotiation skills.

The career management and coaching program doesn't end there. Students receive ongoing career development support through lifetime access to Right Management's career resources, such as an alumni network and a job bank.

The program builds on already-strong career development services at Webster University. These include two programs established in 2013: the Webster mentoring program and Walker EDGE. The Webster mentoring program, offered by the Office of Advancement and the Career Planning and Development Center, connects students with alumni to develop a one-on-one mentoring relationship.

Walker EDGE provides comprehensive professional development resources, programs, and guidance to undergraduate students within the Walker School, including a credit course, internship opportunities, and hybrid courses. Its popular Industry Insight Nights series, which provides opportunities for students to speak and interact with industry professionals and representatives from different St. Louis area companies, is open to both undergraduate and graduate students.

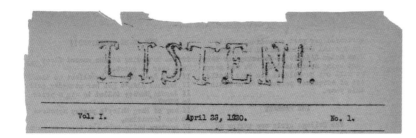

Vol. I.   April 23, 1920.   No. 1.

On April 23, 1920, the first student newspaper, *Listen!*, appeared on the campus of what would become Webster University, almost five years after the founding of the college. The inaugural issue said its purposes included giving students an opportunity to broaden their writing skills.

All students had opportunities to work on *Listen!* because each class of freshmen through seniors took turns producing it. That process, according to an item in the first issue, would "excite a general rivalry and competition as to which class can edit the peppiest paper."

Listen! consisted of one mimeographed page, issued weekly, containing short news and editorial items. The emphasis on editing "the peppiest paper" no doubt accounted for the jokes and poems that also found their way into *Listen!*. News in *Listen!* tended toward coverage of events, athletics, and people at the college

for women. But one memorable editorial in the November 5, 1920, issue rejoiced about "one of the greatest political events of this century"— women voting in a US presidential election for the first time, thanks to gaining their voting rights through the 19th amendment to the U.S. Constitution, ratified in August 1920.

A few years later, what would become the longest-running student newspaper at Webster made its debut: *The Web*, first published on October 3, 1924. *The Web* tied in directly to students studying journalism at Webster as a product of a class taught by Mrs. Daniel Dillon, an experienced journalist. The prodigious contributions of the journalism class and other Webster students led to the newspaper growing to six pages just six months after starting publication.

THE WEB

Vol. 2, No. 1.   WEBSTER COLLEGE   November 2, 1925.

ORGANIZATIONS HOLD GENERAL ELECTIONS	FRESHMEN INVESTED WITH CAPS AND GOWNS	FATHER LORD RATES WEBSTER GIRLS HIGH
Sodality, Classes and Clubs Choose New Officers	Father Donovan Conducts Annual Fall Ceremony	Advises Students to Make the Most of College Careers

The Web would be a staple at Webster until the

end of 1970. It gave experience in real-world journalism for Webster's students, especially those taught by Dillon and her successor, Betty Johnson. In the 1930s, the newspaper would be overseen by longtime faculty member Anna Sankey and *St. Louis Globe-Democrat* reporter Hamilton Thornton. Sankey taught "radio speaking and writing," and Thornton began teaching a journalism course in 1933.

For much of its run, content in *The Web* reflected the times and was a mix of current events, campus news, student humor, and family updates. Articles on the Catholic Church and world affairs shared newspaper space with wedding announcements, news about student club activities, and various jokes about campus life. While some of *The Web*'s material might seem frivolous by later standards, the newspaper was firmly backed by staff and faculty. "We strongly encourage the continuance of *The Web* as a campus newspaper," wrote a faculty member who was less enthusiastic of other Webster student publications of the period.

The unrest that typified the second half of the 1960s showed up in *The Web* stories that addressed the Vietnam War, changing roles for women, and the civil rights movement. The

influx of male students and the transition to a secular institution had a major impact on the newspaper's content.

A short-lived alternative to *The Web* called *The Ster* appeared on October 3, 1966. Its purpose was to provide a second viewpoint "on issues concerning the Webster community. The need for real controversy . . . is a vital part of the motivating force behind this second newspaper." Only a limited number of issues were published, and *The Ster* soon folded.

Two months after *The Web* ceased publication in 1970, an advanced journalism class took up

Don Corrigan

REAL-WORLD JOURNALISM

the cause of a student newspaper at Webster by publishing *The Broadside* in February 1971. Unlike *The Web*, the new publication put its sole focus on journalism. *The Broadside* existed to give students newspaper experience and emphasized straight campus news.

The purpose of providing students with journalism experience was behind the founding of the current Webster newspaper, *The Journal*. Begun as *The Weekly Journal* as a nod to 18th century newspaper pioneer John Peter Zenger and his *New York Weekly Journal*, the new Webster periodical first appeared on September 17, 1976. It became simply *The Journal* starting on February 4, 1977.

Available online as well as in print, *The Journal* remains the major student news organization at Webster University and is consistently recognized in Missouri and nationally as a top college newspaper. In 2015, staff members of *The Journal* received ten Mark of Excellence Awards at the Society of Professional Journalists Region 7 Spring Conference. In addition, for the first time, *The Journal* received the top award for Best All-Around Non-Daily Newspaper.

In 1920, the students who put out the very first student newspaper wondered how their paper would figure in the school's history. It was, in fact, the beginning of a rich tradition which today includes not only print, but broadcast journalism with a unique global perspective. Besides two majors in the subject, students can also earn certificates in specialized areas such as digital media, outdoor/environmental journalism, and magazine production.

For the latter, students have the opportunity to work on the university's student-produced magazine *The Ampersand*. Launched in 2003, *The Ampersand* has won numerous national awards, including the coveted Gold Crown from the Columbia Scholastic Press Association in 2005 and 2010.

The Ampersand is published twice annually by students as part of a senior-level journalism class that awards a magazine production certificate. About a dozen students comprise each class and handle all facets of turning out each issue, including writing, photography, editing, layout, production, and distribution.

The experience of working on *The Ampersand* is one that students carry with them as they move into their careers. "No other university in the area offers this type of educational opportunity," said Alice Telios, one of the editors of the Gold Crown-winning issues in 2009-2010. "*The Ampersand* is one of the reasons why I attended Webster, and it will be one of the reasons why I will visit my alma mater."

Webster University's
student-produced magazine
volume twelve spring 2014

The Journal Newsroom

1926 FORENSICS AND DEBATE

Webster's forensics and debate program carries on a long tradition that began in 1926 with a debate on protective tariffs between an all-female team from Webster and an all-male team from St. Louis University. Webster's women won, establishing a tradition of success that continues to this day.

In the early 1930s, President George Donovan organized weekly debates between juniors and seniors on topics he deemed of interest to Webster's student population. Themes included the League of Nations, the Depression, and the purpose of education. Other debates included topics that hit closer to home, such as this one from 1933: "that students should be permitted to smoke in the college cafeteria."

The current forensics and debate program was established in 1993 and initially coached by Dr. David Harpool, faculty member in the History, Politics and Law Department. For the last twenty years, the program has been led by Scott Jensen, director of forensics and debate and professor in the School of Communications, and Gina Jensen, assistant director of forensics and debate and adjunct professor in the School of Communications.

Open to students from all backgrounds and experience levels, the program offers activities ranging from public speaking opportunities to highly competitive events. Each year, the program holds the Gorlok Gala Invitational, one of the largest tournaments in the Midwest, at the home campus. The 2015 Gala had the biggest turnout in its seventeen-year history, attracting participants from forty-nine schools and twenty-two states.

A further indicator of the forensics and debate program's success is that it qualified students for the elite American Forensic Association National Individual Events Tournament for fifteen consecutive years. Many of the students who participate in debate are majors in speech communication studies, an area that was first offered as a degree in 1934. In those early years, theatre was part of the speech program, and students studied not only voice and diction but also stagecraft, make–up, and costume designing.

Today the degree program offers concentrations in interpersonal/relational communication, professional speaking and performance, and a comprehensive general approach to the field.

Scott Jensen and Gina Jensen (front left) with Debate team, 2013

1931 BROADCASTING

Long before the Internet and television, the dominant broadcast medium was radio, and Webster students have been on the radio since early in the school's history.

In November 1931, a weekly Sunday afternoon show called the *Webster College Hour* began broadcasting over WEW, a St. Louis University-operated station. In that first broadcast, three Webster students discussed unemployment in the United States.

Webster gained its own on-campus radio station, WEBU-AM 660, in 1991. Students in the Communications Department's radio production workshop operated the station in a studio shared with another class in the Sverdrup complex, which limited the station's broadcast time. The station's signal carried only as far as Webster Hall, Maria Hall, and the cafeteria.

A year later, Webster expanded its audience by reaching an agreement to use KSLH, a station owned by the St. Louis Public School Board. The board sold the station in June 1996, however, and Webster once again had to settle for WEBU's limited coverage. WEBU went off the air for good after the spring 1997 semester and came back as KGLX 1220 AM, The Galaxy, on February 2, 1998. It began streaming over the Internet in 2000.

The School of Communications also has provided opportunities for real-world experience in television through Gorlok TV (GTV) which made its debut in January 2003. Some of the early programming featured original shows created by Webster students, including *The Newly-Roomed Show*. Based on the classic television game show *The Newlywed Game*, the GTV version tested college roommates on how well they knew each other. Today GTV features a variety of programming and can be viewed in buildings and student residences on the home campus.

1974

MEDIA COMMUNICATIONS CURRICULUM

In the 1970s, the Media Center served as the home for media studies at Webster. Media Center director Dr. Tom Oates proposed the first undergraduate major in media which was approved in 1974, and barely five years later media studies already had sixty registered majors. In 1978, the Media Center took over the journalism program, formerly part of the Literature and Language Department.

Oates continued to oversee the Media Center and the media studies program until he left in 1981. After his departure, his responsibilities were divided up, and Art Silverblatt was hired to direct the media studies program. Silverblatt was enthusiastic about Webster's curriculum, which balanced theory and practice, adding, "I want the program to produce professionals who can interpret what is going on around us into all areas of the media."

The next fifteen years were a period of growth and expansion. In 1992, a program in interactive media was added, making Webster the first US college to offer a graduate degree in the subject area. An annual awards event called The Webbies (a.k.a. Media Excellence Awards) was begun in the late 1980s and for almost twenty years showcased student work in an expanding number of media areas.

In 1996, the School of Communications was created, which included two departments, Electronic and Photographic Media and Communications and Journalism. A third department, Audio Aesthetics and Technology, was added in 2011.

The fledgling media studies program of the 1970s has grown into a vibrant, diverse home for students studying everything from animation, game design, film, video and audio production, advertising and public relations to journalism, photography, scriptwriting, speech and media communications, and interactive digital media. Besides majors and minors, the school also offers specialized certificates in areas such as documentary production, environmental journalism, commercial photography, and video game foundations.

Art Silverblatt

Julie Griffey

1988 MAY GALLERY AND ELECTRONIC AND PHOTOGRAPHIC MEDIA

It's anyone's guess how many students, faculty, and staff hurry each day through the second-floor corridor at the southern end of the Sverdrup complex on the home campus of Webster University. It may be just a hallway to some, but the area is special to anyone who is an enthusiast of excellent photography. The space marks the School of Communications' May Gallery, one of the few locations in St. Louis dedicated to showing original photography.

The pieces that hang on the wall comprise the work

of photographers who may be internationally known photojournalists, alumni, faculty members, or students. Anyone, in fact, can propose to have an exhibition shown in the May Gallery.

Established in 1988, the May Gallery is open to the public. Professor of photography Bill Barrett directs the May Gallery and curates about eight exhibitions a year, many of them celebrated with opening nights that give visitors a chance to meet the photographers whose works are displayed.

Adjacent to the May Gallery is the Small Wall Gallery, which has shown smaller exhibitions since 2000. An important purpose for both galleries is to serve as an outlet for the work of students from Webster University's global campuses. "My favorite part about the photography program would have to be the studios that we have here. I have access to all kinds of cameras and equipment that are industry-standard and give the students the opportunity to really learn," noted photography major Taylor Ringenberg.

Many of those students are pursuing degrees offered by the Department of Electronic and Photographic Media, an integral part of the School of Communications since its founding in 1996.

The Department of Electronic and Photographic Media offers undergraduate majors, minors, and certificates in a wide range of related fields such as animation, film production, interactive digital media, film studies, photography, and video production. The major fields of study in electronic and photographic media are offered at many of Webster University's global campuses. Students learn real-world techniques through unique, hands-on projects, using professional-grade equipment as early as their freshman year. Their work includes projects for Webster University and outside clients such as non-profit organizations.

Those kinds of experiences "give us the unique opportunity to work on projects for clients that will actually be used," said Jeff G'Sell,

MAY GALLERY AND ELECTRONIC AND PHOTOGRAPHIC MEDIA

Bill Barrett and Eric Rothenbuhler

May Gallery Opening

a student who teamed with his peers to produce professional videos in 2013. "This allows us to have professional video pieces to add to our portfolio, which puts me in a position where I feel more prepared for my future career."

One example of real-world learning is the hands-on experience Webster students are gaining in a show airing on The Nine Network in St. Louis. The show, *Stay Tuned*, has a town hall format and discusses a single issue each week with a host, guests, a studio audience and additional video segments. However, the show differs from traditional town hall formats by incorporating social media into the broadcast, including Facebook, Twitter, and Google+ Hangouts. "Since the show is relatively new, our students have been able to contribute their ideas and try their hand at research, editing, or social media," said Kristen DiFate, assistant professor of digital advertising. "They aren't pigeonholed into one specific task, but they are learning about all aspects of the show's production using the social media channels that are most popular with their peers."

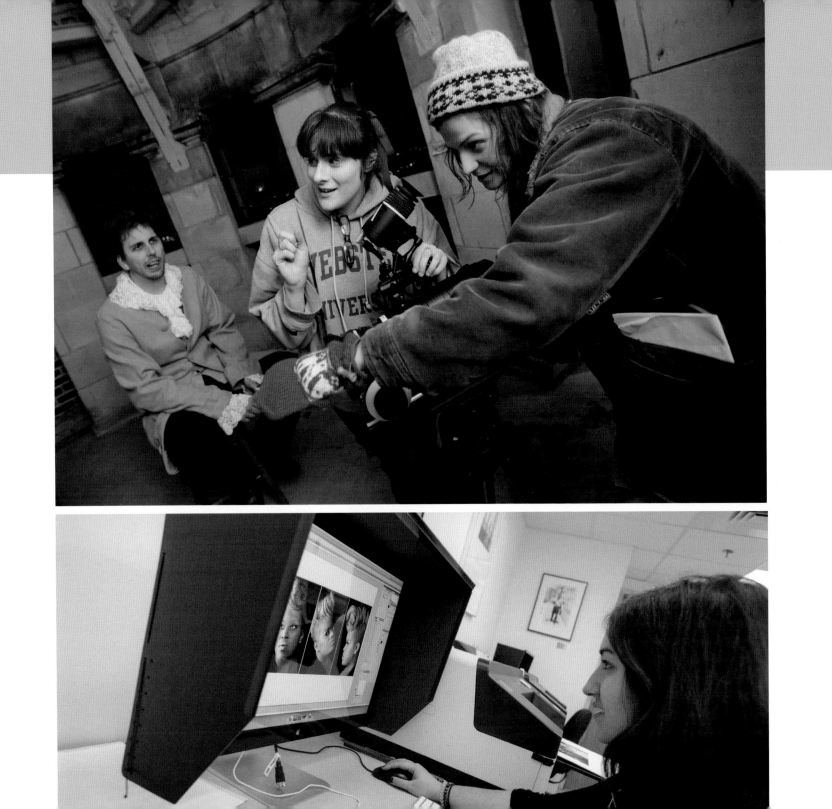

155

Loud sounds, glaringly bright red doors, a leopard skin lamp and a Spinal Tap action figure are just a few of the signs that the audio labs at Webster University's School of Communications offer a slightly different learning experience from what you'd find in the more traditional classrooms down the hall.

"We've worked really hard to create a positive and fun atmosphere," said Barry Hufker, professor and chair of the Department of Audio Aesthetics and Technology. "We try to make it so that from the moment you enter, you feel like this is an exciting, different, and creative place to be."

The program that began twenty-five years ago with only seven students and two small studios in Webster Hall is now the largest in the School of Communications, offering online courses, a focus in international education and an audio recording summer camp for high school students.

The student section of the Audio Engineering Society (AES) has been one of the most active student clubs at Webster. Founded in 2003, the section provides members with invaluable experience and extensive knowledge that richly supplements their coursework.

One of the section's major activities is the AES Central Region Audio Student Summit, held annually at Webster since 2007. The summit was begun as a way to make it easier for students at universities in the Midwest to meet their peers and learn from audio experts in the field. Webster's section of AES also invites internationally known sound experts to speak on campus.

The active nature of the Webster AES chapter is a reflection of the growth in the area of audio production through

the years. During the 1989-90 academic year, an emphasis in audio production was added and by 2000, twelve percent of entering freshmen on the home campus listed audio production as their major. In 2011, a separate department of Audio Aesthetics and Technology was created.

Ken Scott

1990 INTERNSHIP EXPO

"Before this internship, I was nervous about getting my first job out of college, but now I feel so prepared and ready to take on any new challenge that comes my way!"

~ Amanda Karas, SOC student

Every year, SOC students complete credit bearing internships with organizations across the nation. The SOC has over 500 local and national media organizations as educational internship partners. A sample of organizations include: Bruton Stroube Studios, Capital Studios & Mastering, CBS Radio, Chicago Recording Co., Coolfire Media, FOX2/KPLR 11 television, Missouri Botanical Garden, MTV Networks, Nine Network of Public Media, St. Louis Blues, and St. Louis Cardinals. The SOC partners with the Global Internship Experience to provide international internship opportunities for students.

Internships have long been considered an important stepping stone to a career, and nowhere is that more evident than in the School of Communications (SOC). The SOC, in fact, has established a Center for Portfolio Development & Internships for the purpose of helping its students gain valuable real-world experience. As Mindy Berkowitz, center director, states, "I think internships are a great bridge to moving on in your career. They let you see the difference between applying your skills in an academic environment and applying them with actual professionals in the field."

One way the center connects students with host organizations is through the annual Internship Expo, which began in 1990. The Expo typically attracts a variety of organizations ranging from school districts, local municipalities, and nonprofit organizations to studios, magazines, radio stations, and newspapers.

1996 SCHOOL OF COMMUNICATIONS FOUNDED

By 1990, Webster University had developed a plan to reorganize into four schools and colleges . . . or so it seemed. Faculty in the Department of Communications, which would experience forty percent growth in enrollment from 1993-98, sought and gained university-wide support to establish a school for communications. With subsequent approval from the administration, the School of Communications formed under Dean John Neal in 1996.

The School of Communications began with about 200 graduate and undergraduate students in programs offered only at St. Louis. Since then, enrollment has grown to nearly 1,300 in Webster's global network of campuses under Dean Debra Carpenter, who led the school from 1996-2012, and Dean Eric W. Rothenbuhler, who was appointed in 2012.

The school offers degrees at Webster's campuses in Austria, Great Britain, the Netherlands, Switzerland, and Thailand. Plans include adding degree programs at the Ghana and Greece campuses.

The school foresees integrating existing strengths with interconnected, experiential, problem-based learning, using its St. Louis base as the hub of an educational and professional communications network. These plans will be enhanced through a future redesign of the Sverdrup complex, headquarters of the school. Expansive, open entrances and transparent learning areas that will make media and communications work visible are envisioned. The result will invite collaboration among students and faculty working in all modes of communication.

Dean Eric W. Rothenbuehler with students, 2014

2007 ANIMATION AND GAME DESIGN

Frozen, *The Amazing Spider-Man*, *Wolverine*, and *Star Trek Into Darkness* are four of many blockbuster movies that include work from graduates of the School of Communications' animation program.

Webster's animation students integrate content and technique through storytelling skills expressed through current digital animation tools. Established in 2007, the animation program was ranked among the top dozen in the Midwest in 2014.

Kinematifest, a yearly international animation and interactive media festival on the home campus, provides important learning opportunities outside the classroom. Webster's animation students have run the festival since its inception in 2008.

Joining Webster's animation students in a related field for the digital age are those in the School of Communications' bachelor's degree program in game and game design. Building on the certificate program in video game foundations, the school added the degree program in 2014. Students learn theory and design in traditional and video games, then create their own games independently and with teams.

1941 **TEACHER EDUCATION**

The World War II era saw changes in every facet of American life. One of them was a trend toward "professional subjects," which was noted by President George Donovan in his 1941-42 annual report.

It was in that spirit that Webster established a four-year program in elementary education in 1941. Webster had been turning out students who went on to become educators from the school's start, including its very first graduate, Florence Waddock. But the focus on elementary education in 1941 marked the first formal teacher education program at Webster that would lead to today's School of Education.

In the post-war years, teacher education at Webster would transition to a nationally recognized program that fundamentally altered how college students learned to teach. "At the time, teachers stood in front of the class and lectured," said Patricia Chesley Soraghan, class of 1962. "Sr. Jacqueline Grennan wanted Webster to be known for new ways to teach."

Grennan (vice-president and later president of Webster) advocated for educating future teachers "in how to learn as well as how to learn

how to learn." That translated into an emphasis away from teaching methods and toward gaining expertise in a particular subject, which was delivered through experiential learning, or "learning by doing." Webster ceased giving undergraduate degrees in education in 1962, instead requiring students to major in a subject such as mathematics.

"At the same time we began putting an emphasis on content-centered education, we began integrating teacher training into our classes, because most of our students were going to be teachers," recalled Sr. Barbara Ann Barbato. "They were getting both pieces, the material, but also how to teach it."

In the 1960s, Webster offered unique learning opportunities for future teachers. The College School, which opened in 1963, allowed students to work in classrooms conveniently located on the home campus. In addition, Dr. Robert Davis was leading efforts to develop new approaches to teaching mathematics through the Madison Project. Dr. William Walton was also exploring ways to revolutionize science education.

As students completed their studies and began teaching throughout the region, school superintendents were so impressed with these graduates that they asked Webster to develop

TEACHER EDUCATION

a similar graduate-level curriculum for veteran educators. Webster responded by starting the master of arts in teaching, the school's first graduate program, in 1964. "What we are today began in 1964, with an advanced program for certified elementary school teachers who wanted to deepen their content knowledge," said Dr. Brenda Fyfe, dean of the School of Education (SOE).

In the decades that followed, Webster's teacher education program continued to respond to changing times, such as by developing courses on the early adolescent learner and early childhood education. Fyfe has also been instrumental in introducing the education practices of the Reggio Emilia approach not only to Webster students but to teachers in the St. Louis area.

Today SOE master's and undergraduate programs encompass more than a dozen areas of concentration offered at the home campus, Kansas City, and online. All of the School of Education's degrees are accredited by the National Council for

Accreditation of Teacher Education and the Missouri Department of Elementary and Secondary Education.

Webster University's tradition of producing teachers of the highest quality has been widely recognized. Accolades include those earned by Margaret Williams, Missouri Teacher of the Year in 2009, and Kristen Merrell, who received the same award in 2011.

TEACHER EDUCATION

Imagine asking a group of third grade students to find the height of a flagpole and leaving them to figure out how to do so. Such a task may seem too much to ask of children this age, but it was precisely this type of problem solving that was commonly found in a Madison Project classroom.

The Madison Project, a different approach to learning and teaching math, was brought to Webster College in 1961 by Sr. Jacqueline Grennan, then Webster's vice president of development. She believed the Madison Project would fit well with Webster's undergraduate

teacher-education program, which with the help of a grant from the Ford Foundation, was developing a content-centered curriculum with particular emphasis in the areas of math, science, and foreign languages. In 1961, Grennan tendered a position to Dr. Robert Davis, who led the Madison Project at Syracuse University, and invited him to base the project at Webster.

Davis' approach to mathematics fit well with Webster's philosophy regarding teacher education. As he stated a year after his arrival: "There is great emphasis on making children understand what they are doing and why they are doing it. This demands more skill, training, and effort on the teacher's part than the traditional approach, in which children are taught rules and techniques without, oftentimes, being told why . . . We want the class situation to be a lively experience, not sterile or pedantic. Having specialists in the class room engenders a good deal of this aura of excitement."

Besides teaching at Webster, Davis took the Madison Project into a number of St. Louis elementary schools. He also held workshops for teachers in local school districts and received funding to produce movies of Madison Project techniques being used with schoolchildren.

At Webster, Davis and the Madison Project "had an electrifying influence on the training of prospective elementary teachers," recalled Anna Barbara Sakurai, who joined Webster's faculty in 1963. "The project was an enormous boost for Webster." As those students graduated and taught successfully using Davis' methods, Webster acquired a reputation as a leader in teacher education. Peg Jostedt, class of 1947, summed up Webster's innovative approach to program development by stating "I don't know of any other college in the country doing a more vital job of meeting the responsibilities of our changing world."

Long after the funded project ended, the Madison Project's legacy lives on in contemporary math education circles. According to Carol Schwab, associate professor in math & computer science, "current teaching materials, including the Common Core State Standards, are permeated by ideas and ideals from Dr. Davis and the Madison Project." In addition, books by Marilyn Burns, perhaps Davis' most well-known protégé, are still used today.

Robert Davis

1963 THE COLLEGE SCHOOL

A wealth of new ideas in learning and teacher education flooded Webster College in the 1960s. The Webster-based Madison Project was at the forefront of the new math movement to better educate elementary school students in mathematics. Meanwhile, Webster changed the way its student teachers learned by requiring them to major in a specific subject instead of general teacher education.

It was in this spirit of educational innovation that Webster opened The College School in September 1963.

Temporarily located in two mobile homes on the St. Louis campus, The College School served as a training ground for Webster's students and faculty to teach elementary pupils. As a press release put it, "The inductive approach in the learning process, stressed by Jerome Bruner of Harvard, will penetrate the total curriculum."

Nelson Haggerson, the first director, described The College School "as a laboratory for trying new materials and methods of teaching . . . a laboratory for Webster College faculty involved in teacher education to be directly involved in experimentation with students and real school situations." He went on to write that lessons learned from The College School would be incorporated into Webster's teacher education programs.

The College School flaunted convention by doing things such as teaching economics, French, and music to first-grade students. Faculty member Anna Barbara Sakurai developed a non-denominational religion program. "I was amazed at how lively religion classes could be when students could share ideas with children of different backgrounds than their own," she said.

Webster intended for The College School to be a short-term project and planned to end it after the spring, 1967 semester. But under pressure from parents and faculty, The College School continued. Housed in what is today's visual arts studios, the school remained part of Webster until 1979.

The College School continues as an independent institution less than a mile from the Webster campus. Today, Webster University and The College School continue to partner in mutually beneficial ways, including experiential learning, student teacher practicums, conferences, grant projects, and sustainability collaborations.

1964 MASTER OF ARTS IN TEACHING

Webster University did not offer graduate degrees during its first forty-nine years of existence. That changed with the launching of the master of arts in teaching (MAT) in 1964.

By 1963, Webster's innovative undergraduate program had caught the attention of educators and media. Rather than train its students in how to teach by traditional methods, Webster emphasized "learning how to learn" by majoring in a subject, such as mathematics or science, and delivering classes in those subjects by using simple materials to teach children. For example, young children learned addition and subtraction by putting stones in, and taking them out of, paper bags.

The Saturday Evening Post praised Webster's teacher education program in one of its 1963 issues. Meanwhile, Webster's students were putting into practice what they had learned through student teaching in local schools. The student teachers were so impressive that superintendents of three St. Louis school districts requested an MAT program at Webster for their current teachers.

Webster first offered the MAT with classes in

science, mathematics, and foreign languages in the summer of 1964.

The same concepts learned by Webster's undergraduates were taught to MAT participants, and the outcomes could be dramatic. The MAT program "saved me from leaving teaching," said Carolyn Cottrell, class of 1969. "I was not having a good time teaching history to eighth graders. The MAT program put way more tools in my toolbox. I got it—I understood the conceptual approach to teaching. It turned out I loved eighth graders."

By the time Cottrell enrolled in the MAT, participation had reached 450, more than half of Webster's total enrollment. In 1972, Webster opened its first metro campus in Kansas City— which Cottrell later directed—to deliver the MAT program.

The early MAT would be the start of greatly expanded programs in the School of Education. Today, it offers thirty master's degrees, specialist degrees, certificates, and, most recently, a doctor of education in transformative learning in the global community.

Bill McConnell
and students

1977 AT THE FOREFRONT OF PERSONAL COMPUTING

As personal computers began to appear in the 1970s, the education faculty helped Webster launch the first courses on microcomputers in Missouri. Dr. Andrea Rothbart, who taught mathematics in Webster's teacher education program, worked with Dr. Ed Sakurai, chair of the Mathematics Department, to bring those first computers to Webster in 1977.

A few years later, Webster began a program for elementary and middle school teachers that taught them how to use computers in their classrooms. Webster's MAT faculty also introduced the computer language LOGO into the graduate curriculum.

In the 1990s, the School of Education (SOE) took a leading role as Webster capitalized on new opportunities made possible by the Internet. In 1997, the school introduced a course called technology in the classroom, which combined coursework and practice teaching in a Webster Groves school district classroom. According to Dr. Paul Steinmann, professor of education, teachers needed to know how to use the Internet because "in the next five to ten years, the Internet will be the greatest resource that a classroom teacher will have."

In 1999, SOE offered two of Webster's first online degree programs, an MAT in multidisciplinary studies and an MAT in educational technology. Response from students was immediately and overwhelmingly positive. "Online courses seem to sell themselves," wrote Dr. Roy Tamashiro and Frances Erwin shortly after the online degree program began. Currently the SOE offers a number of master's and educational specialist degrees online.

Almost forty years ago, students came to Webster to take that first education course on microcomputers. Today, the School of Education is bringing high-quality education programs to students via the convenience of Internet access.

Alaa Abudarb remembers his struggles in school as a ten-year-old immigrant from Iraq. "I felt I was lost, especially during test time," he said.

As a Webster University student in 2012, Abudarb found a way to ensure that others didn't have that experience. He joined the Student Literacy Corps (SLC), established by the forerunner of the School of Education in 1990.

Established to give education majors teaching experience while helping struggling readers in schools across St. Louis, the SLC continues a tradition of service begun by the Loretto Community, which founded Webster University. The SLC, along with programs such as Webster Works Worldwide, earned Webster a place on the

President's Higher Education Community Service Honor Roll in 2014.

The SLC celebrated its twenty-fifth anniversary in 2015. The program attracts student tutors from throughout the university and now trains math tutors as well. In recent years, Webster international students have enjoyed special success working with immigrant and refugee families at schools and community centers that focus on the needs of English language learners. Through the SLC, Webster trains and supervises between forty and sixty tutors annually, who

work with over 1,000 learners in St. Louis schools, homeless shelters, and adult education centers. Principals and teachers report their students have increased confidence, motivation, and success thanks to their SLC tutors.

Student Centered Learning in the Disciplines: Education

Dean Brenda Fyfe
with students, 2014

1995 SCHOOL OF EDUCATION FOUNDED

While teacher education has been a key element of Webster University since its start, the formation of the School of Education (SOE) happened eighty years after Webster opened as Loretto College.

Webster formed the SOE as part of a general reorganization that began in the mid-1980s. In what undergraduate dean Dr. Neil George would later describe as a faculty-driven process, discussions over the next few years established the composition of what would become today's five schools and colleges at Webster. The School of Education was formed in August 1995 under acting dean Dr. Brenda Fyfe, who was followed by Dr. Judith Walker de Felix.

Fyfe described a multitude of benefits for students in the establishment of the School of Education: "What will change is the quality of programming, the direction of school activities, and the visibility of the school in the community and internally."

Fyfe returned to teaching after serving as acting dean. She was named dean in 2003. Under her leadership, the school has achieved many milestones, including national specialized accreditation, the largest grant awarded to the university, and the development of the university's second doctoral degree, a doctor of education in transformative learning in the global community.

1999 KORNBLUM INSTITUTE

Brenda Fyfe, Beatrice Kornblum, and Jacqueline Grennan Wexler

Established in 1999 by a $2.4 million gift from Beatrice Kornblum, the institute supports innovative education, program development, community service, and improved teaching and learning, with emphasis on disadvantaged urban children.

Kornblum worked with Dr. Brenda Fyfe, then a teaching professor in the School of Education and now dean of the school, to lay the groundwork for the institute. Together, they developed plans to fund full scholarships to graduate students who were practicing teachers, to integrate arts into education, and to provide services for disadvantaged children.

Those plans and Kornblum's donation enabled the School of Education to begin programs it otherwise could not have afforded. "Many of the ideas in the institute are the kinds of ideas that have been discussed in the department before the funding was available," Fyfe said.

The School of Education carries on the life's work of Beatrice Kornblum, a dedicated St. Louis schoolteacher, through the Beatrice and David Kornblum Institute for Teaching Excellence.

Kornblum, who was ninety-three at the time of her donation, became familiar with Webster through her friendship with Fyfe. Kornblum was impressed by Webster's internationalism and dedicated faculty, even though she never attended the school. At the time, her gift was the largest by an individual to Webster.

"I want to encourage new teachers who are in impoverished conditions to go on with their studies so they can go on with helping their students," Kornblum said.[25]

The Kornblum Institute has made her wishes come true by sponsoring a variety of programs and activities. In addition to preparing School of Education students for teaching disadvantaged children, the institute funds lectures by visiting scholars, seminars on topics such as civil rights, and student research to develop papers presented at major conferences.

Brenda Fyfe, Des Lee, and Carla Rinaldi

Janaki Rajan

Webster University's efforts to bring a global perspective into every classroom took a major step forward in 2001 when the School of Education welcomed Dr. Carla Rinaldi as Webster's first Des Lee International Scholar.

Rinaldi, an internationally renowned early childhood educator and professor and president of Reggio Children in Reggio Emilia, Italy, taught in the School of Education in the fall of 2001. She brought ideas such as the Reggio Emilia Approach, an educational philosophy to realize children's strong potential for development, to students in the School of Education.

Established through the support of St. Louis philanthropist Des Lee, the program brought an internationally known scholar each year to teach in one of Webster University's five schools and colleges. The Des Lee International Scholars program ran until 2011 and culminated with Dr. Janaki Rajan, who taught in the School of Education in 2011. Rajan is an Indian educator active in child rights, women's and girls' rights movements, and the reform of the Indian school system.

2012 U.S. DEPARTMENT OF EDUCATION GRANT

The School of Education (SOE) is meeting the needs of an increasingly diverse American society through a five-year program established by a $1.9 million grant from the U.S. Department of Education in 2012.

With the largest federal grant in Webster's history, the SOE established a program that trains current teachers in Kansas City to create a better learning environment for students from immigrant families where at least one other language besides English is spoken. One in four children in America, and about forty percent of students in the Kansas City Missouri School District, fall into that category.

The program takes eighteen months to complete and results in earning an English speakers of other languages certificate from Webster University. About 100 teachers will earn certificates over the five-year life of the program. They will take their new-found expertise back to their schools with a goal of creating a better learning environment for Kansas City's students.

President Stroble and Dean Fyfe

Rudolph Torrini

The tradition of art at Webster University reaches deep into the school's past. Art, in fact, was one of sixteen classes listed in the first course catalog published by the school. Webster offered its first major in art in the mid-1940s. Kathlyn Hammes and Patricia Willet became Webster's first graduates with art majors in 1948.

Webster added a second major in arts in 1975 by establishing the bachelor of fine arts (BFA) degree. The BFA's purposes were to emphasize art skills development and to qualify graduates for master's programs requiring BFA degrees.

Students enrolled in the BFA and other art programs at Webster did much of their work in the Thompson Carriage House, the home of the Art Department, beginning in the 1960s. The Art Department moved to its current home in the visual arts studios in 1988. In 1991, the building added a sculpture studio with soaring ceilings and a clerestory.

Today, the Department of Art, Design and Art History (DADAH) prepares students to successfully encounter the art world by encouraging them to understand and synthesize traditions and to confront challenging ideas and emerging technologies. DADAH offers undergraduate students the option to work toward one of three core degrees. Two of them are bachelor of arts degrees in art and art history and criticism. The third is a bachelor of fine arts in art with an emphasis in studio art or graphic design. While all three are traditional degrees, the paths to them exemplify the uniqueness of DADAH.

DADAH's faculty members establish a learning plan for each incoming student based on the student's portfolio, experience, and expectations. Those students become part of a culture deliberately intended to be informal, familial, inclusive, inspiring, and supportive. It's also a culture with high expectations for hard work, intensive study, and project involvement. Students attend classes, but only on Mondays through Thursdays. Fridays are reserved for projects. The visual arts studios on the St. Louis campus never close, and students can be seen anytime of the day or night in studios and labs expressing themselves through anything from paintings, drawings and sculptures, as well as experiments with sound and light.

The visual arts studios are filled with their work, some of which can be displayed in the Cecille R. Hunt Gallery, which opened in 1983 and is directed by professor of art history & criticism Jeffrey Hughes. The gallery presents works of regionally, nationally, and internationally prominent artists in non-commercial, professionally curated exhibitions

Tom Lang

ART

open to the public. The gallery is named for Cecille Hunt, a dedicated supporter of the arts in St. Louis and Washington, DC, who died in 1981.

Today, DADAH provides a variety of programs that cover the gamut from high school to graduate studies. Each summer, DADAH presents Hands-On Art Training, a nine-day institute for high school students. For undergraduates, DADAH offers minors in art, graphic design, and art history and criticism and certificates in art therapy, international art studies and curatorial studies in addition to its three core undergraduate degrees. Graduate students can pursue a master of arts in art with emphasis in studio art or art history and criticism. The emphasis in studio art is an initial professional degree, while the emphasis in art history and criticism prepares students for doctoral programs or the art museum and gallery professions.

DADAH encourages all of its students to take advantage of the many opportunities for international study

Carol Hodson

Hunt Gallery
Exhibition

available at Webster University to gain greater insight by studying global artwork in situ. In line with Webster's focus on global citizenship, study abroad opens students to different cultures and the myriad values, beliefs, insights, and relationships consonant with such exposure. Such understanding can help provide even further insight into artworks under study. In addition, DADAH offers experiences specifically related to art history at Webster's London location, and biennial, alternating, short-term study abroad trips to Florence and to Venice.

Exceptional learning and performance opportunities delivered by leading educational figures and professional practitioners are the hallmarks of the highly regarded Department of Music in the Leigh Gerdine College of Fine Arts. In 1916, the university opened in St. Louis with a Music Department headed by Sr. Mary Borgia Clarke. The college's eight faculty members included two dedicated to piano and vocal instruction.

Almost from the start, the department provided performance opportunities and professional events. A school orchestra formed in 1931 and played at various assemblies and graduation exercises. The Music Department sponsored numerous events headlined by leading musicians and conductors such as Rudolph Ganz, conductor of the St. Louis Symphony Orchestra from 1921-1927, and Felix Slatkin, violinist and conductor of the 20th Century Fox studio orchestra during the 1940s.

The first formal music education program at Webster made its debut as an undergraduate minor in 1943. Music also figured in two other milestones in Webster history. The school's first African-American graduate (Janet Irene Thomas, class of 1950) and one of the first male graduates

Sr. Eloise Jarvis

(James Ryan, class of 1964) both majored in music.

The Department of Music has been accredited by the National Association of Schools of Music since 1952. Music education gained momentum in the 1960s and 1970s. The Webster Symphony Orchestra, which mixed professionals with students, began a forty-five-year run in 1967. A decade later, the Department of Music launched its first graduate degree program. Approved

in 1976, the new master of music degree focused on performance and pedagogy.

A key development in the story of the Department of Music unfolded in 1997 with the forging of a partnership with the St. Louis Symphony Orchestra.

The partnership started graduate programs in the department for musicians and conductors that featured opportunities to study and perform with the symphony. The agreement also opened a Webster University branch of the St. Louis Symphony Music School, which had been delivering music lessons in St. Louis since 1925.

One outcome of the partnership was completely unexpected. In 2001, financial issues led to the symphony's decision to cease running its music school. Webster University took over the music school's entire operations, renaming it the Community Music School (CMS) of Webster University. President Richard Meyers called the CMS "a stunning addition to the university."

The CMS has become an important element of Webster's commitment to music education. A faculty that includes

MUSIC

members of the St. Louis Symphony Orchestra and instructors from Webster teaches students of all ages and abilities. The school is headquartered in a building that opened on the St. Louis campus in 2006. The facility features a 470-seat concert hall, fifteen teaching studios, two large rehearsal halls, and administrative offices.

The addition of the CMS opened a new path of important advances in music education at Webster. They included designation of Webster University as an All-Steinway School in 2010. Awarded by Steinway and Sons, world-renowned makers of high quality pianos, the All-Steinway designation signifies first-class status for music schools. Webster became the fourth school in Missouri, and 123rd in the world, to receive the designation, which was made possible by President Stroble and Provost Schuster through strategic initiatives funds.

During their course of study, music majors enjoy a wealth of opportunities to learn and to perform. Twelve full-time faculty members and more than sixty adjunct artists and instructors provide private lessons and teach in the classroom. Music majors can study in Vienna during their junior year. Five choral, five instrumental, and three jazz student ensembles perform locally and regionally. The Opera Studio of Webster University provides performance training in conjunction with the professional Opera Theatre of Saint Louis and the Repertory Theatre of St. Louis, both based at the St. Louis campus.

Trent Patterson (far right) with the Webster University Chamber Singers, 2013

MUSIC

Many graduates have established successful careers in music. Alumni include Douglas Major, head of the music program at the National Cathedral in Washington, DC, and the 2013 Outstanding Alumnus of the Leigh Gerdine College of Fine Arts. Jennifer Johnson Cano performs as a member of the Metropolitan Opera. Composer and performer John Zorn received the 2006 MacArthur Foundation Fellowship and the American Academy of Arts and Letters 2012 Arts and Letters Award in Music.

The Webster University Chamber Singers, one of five choral ensembles sponsored by the Department of Music, is widely recognized for its excellence in performance. The ensemble tours annually and represents the department and university at regional events, such as the Southwestern Divisional American Choral Directors Association and the Missouri Music Educators Association. In addition, the ensemble is sought after to perform at major venues such as the Sheldon Concert Hall and the Pulitzer Foundation for the Arts. For

The Marriage of Figaro

the re-opening of the latter in 2015, the ensemble sang a newly commissioned choral work. Chair of the Department of Music Jeffrey Carter noted: "It is an honor to have so many members of the Department of Music's community selected to participate in the re-opening of a nationally recognized gallery space. This is a unique musical piece that will give our students and faculty a live experience that may never be duplicated again. It is a once-in-a-lifetime opportunity."

Recognition earned by the Chamber Singers caps a century of achievement for music education at Webster University. The future is just as bright. Outstanding alumni and highly regarded educational programs in music demonstrate a commitment to musical excellence that runs throughout the historical fabric of Webster University.

Along with its established education and performance programs, Webster continues to innovate through new undergraduate degree offerings in songwriting and musical theatre directing. Combining a global perspective with high quality educational experiences, the Department of Music is well-positioned to continue its mission of educating vibrant artists and teachers for successful careers worldwide.

1925 DANCE

The Department of Dance continues a tradition nearly as old as Webster University itself of developing performers, choreographers, and educators.

Beginning with the school's first-known dance classes in 1925 and continuing with modern dance courses in the 1940s, dance at Webster gained momentum with the establishment of a program emphasizing creative choreography in 1964. In the fall of 1973, Webster Dance Theater, a performing company of ten students, was formed to open the way toward a major in dance. Approval was given for a major in dance the following year.

Dance continued to thrive under program director Ann Vashon and later Gary Hubler. In 1982, the department was renamed the Theatre and Dance Department. In 1993, a bachelor of fine arts degree in dance was established. Seven years later, the program moved into a new home in the Loretto-Hilton Center for the Performing Arts: the Jean and Wells Hobler Center for Dance, made possible by an $800,000 gift from the Hoblers. The gift enabled the creation of two dance studios and supporting facilities.

Growth of the dance and theatre programs led to the separation of the departments in 2010. "It makes sense to ensure the dance department has identification of its own," said Peter Sargent, dean of the Leigh Gerdine College of Fine Arts. "Students coming into the school should know it's a major department."

Today, the Department of Dance offers bachelor of fine arts degrees in dance with emphasis in either ballet or modern, a bachelor of arts degree in dance with ballet or modern emphasis, and minors in dance technique and dance theory. Dance students benefit from witnessing and working with performing arts professionals from around the country in the Loretto-Hilton Center for the Performing Arts. Webster's dancers also partner with other professional dance companies and arts organizations in St. Louis.

Beckah Reed

Jerry Mitchell

Student Centered Learning in the Disciplines: Fine Arts

Sr. Marita Michenfelder with students

Shakespeare Pilgrimage

Hunter Bell, Norbert Leo Butz, Jay Heiserman, Marsha Mason, and Jerry Mitchell have received the entertainment industry's highest awards. They share one other characteristic: They are alumni of the Conservatory of Theatre Arts in the Leigh Gerdine College of Fine Arts. When they reflect on their careers, they point to the conservatory as critical to their success.

"Marita Woodruff and Wayne Loui, two of my teachers there, were my greatest influences," said Mason (class of 1964), Emmy and Academy Award nominee and two-time Golden Globe winner.[26]

"When I first got to Webster, there was a man in charge of acting, Michael Pierce," said two-time Tony winner Butz (class of 1990). "He was, and still is, the greatest teacher I ever had. That's the class that really grabbed me, and I've not stopped pursuing acting since."

The conservatory has been grabbing promising students and turning them into successful artists for a half century. That success stems from excellent teachers and a program unique among the conservatory's peers.

"One of the distinguishing elements of the conservatory is its integrated association with

Norbert Leo Butz (left) and
Frank Van Bree in *The Normal Heart*

professional theatre companies," said Dottie Marshall Englis, chair of the conservatory. "We also enjoy a one-of-a-kind association with a professional musical theatre. These partnerships provide students with unique opportunities in performance and production unequaled at any other undergraduate institution. To witness the best of the profession producing exceptional theatre close up is a rare opportunity."

Conservatory students work hand-in-hand with The Repertory Theatre of St. Louis and Opera Theatre of Saint Louis, two professional performing companies that share the Loretto-Hilton Center for the Performing Arts with the conservatory. The conservatory provides further opportunities for its students through partnerships with The Muny, America's oldest and largest outdoor musical theatre, and the annual Shakespeare Festival St. Louis.

The conservatory's theatre education programs continue a longstanding tradition at Webster University. That tradition began as early as 1917, when the Loretto Players performed their first play, *The Ladies of Cranford*. In 1928, the Loretto Players gave the first-ever "masked" play in St. Louis, combining pantomime and modern dance.

Wayne Loui in
*Stop the World,
I Want to Get Off*

Peter DeFaria (left) and
Rocky Carroll in *Othello*

CONSERVATORY OF THEATRE ARTS

For much of the early 20th century, drama at Webster was under the direction of the brother-and-sister team of Harry R. McClain and Anna McClain Sankey. Harry McClain served as a faculty member in the Speech Department, the original home of the theatre program, and taught at Webster until 1954. Sankey headed Webster's Speech Department for many years and also left Webster in the early 1950s.

McClain is credited with initiating the annual pilgrimage to the Shakespeare statue in Tower Grove Park in St. Louis. Starting in 1939 and lasting for the next fifteen years, this event brought the community together for speeches, a scene from a Shakespeare play performed by Webster students, and often guest appearances (including by well-known actors such as Vincent Price and Helen Hayes).

A major turning point in the history of theatre at Webster came when one of Harry McClain's former students, Sr. Marita Michenfelder (later Marita Woodruff), took over what was then the Speech and Drama Department in 1957. Sr. Marita played a pivotal role in the growth of theatre at Webster. In 1962, she and fellow faculty member Wayne Loui started Theatre Impact, a Webster

College troupe which presented outdoor summertime productions on the home campus and later in nearby Kirkwood Park. The company featured professional actors and Webster students, including Marsha Mason.

At the same time, Webster was building the Loretto-Hilton Center for the Performing Arts, the first in the United States to be designed as home of a professional acting company and an undergraduate theatre arts department. When the center opened in 1966, Theatre Impact, under the new name of the Repertory Theatre of St. Louis, took up residence in the Loretto-Hilton. The Rep, as it came to be called, produced five plays in its initial season with professional actors and Webster students. Due to financial difficulties, the company suspended operations in the early 1970s and soon reopened as a non-profit organization independent of the university. The Rep and the conservatory, however, maintained their partnership, which continues to offer high quality educational experiences to today's theatre students.

Webster's conservatory deserves credit for a number of noteworthy productions through the years. In 1972, a production of *Picnic*, directed

CONSERVATORY OF THEATRE ARTS

Mary Alice Dwyer
in *Matchmaker*

by Marita Michenfelder, won the regional competition of the American Theatre Arts Festival. In 1986, Larry Kramer's groundbreaking play about the AIDS epidemic, *The Normal Heart*, made its St. Louis debut at Webster. In 2002, theatre goers had the chance to see the musical *Pippin,* directed and choreographed by Louise Quick, a member of the original Broadway production.

Perhaps no one else knows the conservatory better than Peter Sargent, dean of the Leigh Gerdine College of Fine Arts, who started as a lighting designer in the conservatory in 1966. "Working with the kind of students we get, I can't help but be excited about the future. We're getting such amazingly talented young artists. That's what keeps you young."

Today's conservatory continues Webster's longstanding tradition of theatre excellence. Programs in performance, stage management, theatre studies and dramaturgy, design, and technical production train young artists for the theatre. Webster's 2015 commencement speaker, acclaimed actress, singer, and community activist Jenifer Lewis, exemplifies the service and career achievements of conservatory alumni.

Dunsi Dai

Marsha Mason
in *Electra*

Midsummer Nights Dream

Into the Woods

1994 COLLEGE OF FINE ARTS FOUNDED

Over the years, Webster's administrative structure has changed to reflect the growth and expansion of the university. Where once there was a single administrator overseeing the academic offerings of the young college, today there are department chairs, deans, a provost, and a vice provost responsible for an impressive array of liberal arts and professional programs.

The fine arts area is a perfect example of the changes that have occurred over time. Since the early years of the university, students have been studying art, music, dance, and theatre. In time, art and music became their own departments, along with what was known as "theatre arts." Dance was included with the latter, and the name would be changed to the Theatre and Dance Department in 1982. Dance would later become its own department in 2010.

By the early 1990s, Webster's fine arts programs in theatre, dance, music, and art were firmly established and attracting students from around the world. The acting program alone conducted auditions for about a thousand applicants each year for just thirty spaces. Accordingly, academic dean Dr. Neil George included the College of Fine

Arts as one of the schools and colleges to form during a reorganization of Webster University. University trustees gave their approval for a College of Fine Arts in 1994.

Peter E. Sargent has been an integral part of Webster's fine arts programs since 1966, when he joined the Conservatory of Theatre Arts as a lighting designer and later became chair of theatre arts and associate dean of fine arts. Affectionately known as "the man in plaid" for his affinity for plaid sports coats, Sargent took the reins of the new college as acting dean in 1994 and dean a year later.

In September 2000, the College of Fine Arts became the first named school or college in Webster's history when it was named for former president Dr. Leigh Gerdine. Gerdine, an accomplished musician, Rhodes Scholar, and former chair of the music department at Washington University, came to Webster in 1970 and served as president for 20 years. He was known not only for what he accomplished at Webster but for the pivotal role he played in revitalizing the Repertory Theatre of St. Louis, the founding of Opera Theatre of Saint Louis and the restoration of the Sheldon Concert Hall.

Today the Leigh Gerdine College of Fine Arts, called "a premier college for the arts," is known not only for its gifted graduates but for its equally gifted faculty. Students learn alongside working actors, musicians, dancers, and artists, and display their talents in numerous exhibits, concerts, and productions throughout the year.

Dean Peter E. Sargent with students, 2014

1916 FIRST SPORTS TEAM

"The unbounded enthusiasm that the College girls are showing in basket-ball and tennis is indeed remarkable."

~ Listen! *Loretto College newspaper, 1920*

Sports at Loretto College began with the appearance of the basketball team in November 1916. In just a few years, students also were playing tennis on courts behind Webster Hall and competing in track and field during springtime Field Days.

That led to the founding of the Athletic Association in 1919 and the opening in 1920 of the Idle Hour gym across Plymouth Avenue from Webster Hall. Idle Hour also held numerous social functions. That explained the fireplace in the wall behind one basket, adding new meaning to the term "hot shooter."

Webster's early teams played against other local colleges and in intramurals. Webster even had a world-class athlete, Elizabeth Wilde, who represented the United States in the 1932 Olympics and finished sixth in the 100-meter dash.[27] She enrolled at Webster the autumn after the Olympics and graduated in 1936.

Today, Webster offers a full array of team sports, including basketball, cross country, soccer, tennis, and track & field for men and women; softball, volleyball, and competitive cheerleading for women; and baseball and golf for men.

IDLE HOUR GYMNASIUM
WEBSTER COLLEGE

Webster Groves Campus

FRESHIES

Thailand Campus

1918 NEW STUDENT ORIENTATION

Geneva Campus

"Scarcely had we adjusted ourselves to the routine of the school year, when the Freshies were put through the usual initiation ceremony."

~ Lorettine, 1921

Today's annual August weekend of new student orientation at Webster University hearkens back to a tradition started in the school's early days as Loretto College.

In the early years, orientation activities were mainly social, with picnics and dinners and tours of St. Louis. A cryptic initiation ceremony for freshmen in 1918 is mentioned, but no details are given as ". . . no loyal member of the College would ever upon any condition whatsoever reveal to anyone their awful mysteriousness." By the 1920s some good-natured hazing was the norm, including administering "a flour and water face-pack and a cold-coffee shampoo" to blindfolded freshmen, who had to wear white baby bibs until Thanksgiving and were forbidden to use the elevator until Christmas.

By the 1940s and 1950s, orientation week featured a full schedule of speakers, entrance exams, and classes, in addition to social activities such as pajama parties, dinners, and fashion shows. A Student Orientation Service was begun to supplement a Big Sister-Little Sister program and aid freshmen in adjusting to college life. Later a bit of fun was had at the freshmen's expense as a green beanie was introduced, and wearing it was mandatory until Halloween.

Initiation rituals have evolved over the decades into today's orientations that integrate new students and parents into campus life at Webster University throughout its worldwide network.

Growing School Spirit

Helen Manion, 1951

"I am honored and excited to serve as the new Athletics Director at Webster University. We have outstanding, amazing student-athletes, coaches, and staff who work hard every day to continue the proud tradition of Gorlok Athletics. One of the most memorable moments this year was the presentation of the inaugural "Athletics Pioneer Award" to Ms. Helen Manion Comer, (class of 1951) at the Gorlok Hall of Fame Ceremony. She is an amazing person who helped pave the way for our student-athletes to compete at the NCAA level."

~ Director of the Athletics Program, 2015, Scott Kilgallon

Webster students have been playing basketball, tennis, and a variety of other sports since the school was founded, but today's athletics program didn't begin until 1984. Much of the credit for bringing intercollegiate sports and the school spirit they create to Webster University belongs to alumnus and Webster staff member Niel DeVasto.

A year after graduating from Webster, DeVasto returned to work in admissions in 1980. The school had no intercollegiate sports program, and DeVasto saw that as a disadvantage in recruiting high school students.

He proposed a sports program in 1983, gained approval in 1984, and received authority to put

the program together. Webster's first teams competed in the National Little College Athletic Association while seeking entry into the National Collegiate Athletic Association (NCAA). Webster began competing in NCAA Division III in 1986.

In 1989, DeVasto approached other nearby schools to form an NCAA Division III athletic conference. The St. Louis Intercollegiate Athletic Conference (SLIAC) began in 1990 with Webster and five other schools as charter members.[28] The women's volleyball team won Webster's first SLIAC championship in 1994,[29] and Webster's men's and women's teams have gone on to capture the second-highest all-time total of SLIAC titles.[30]

1984 BIRTH OF THE GORLOK

"We started the [athletic] program from literally nothing in the spring of '84. One thing we didn't have was a mascot. . . . We took a vote and, son of a gun, Gorlok won."

~ *Sports Information Director Niel DeVasto*[31]

In a world of Tigers and Lions and Bears, Webster University went where no one had gone before when it hit upon the Gorlok as the school's symbol in 1984.

U.S. News & World Report has ranked the Gorlok among the top ten weirdest mascots in the United States.[32] It has finished as the top vote-getter in a "Mascot Madness" competition held by a radio station in Tucson, Arizona.

Until 1984, no college could claim the Gorlok because it is a figment of Webster students' imaginations. Named for the intersection of Gore and Lockwood Avenues near Webster's home campus, the Gorlok was given the paws of a cheetah, the horns of a buffalo, and the face of a Saint Bernard. Student Larry Underwood drew

the first Gorlok with a mustache, a cigar, and a pump-spray insect repellent.[33]

The Gorlok's design has been revised through the years, but the mascot that distinguishes Webster University from all others continues to confound college sports traditionalists. In 2014, Webster's Student Government Association and Student Ambassadors launched a student-led fundraising initiative aimed at installing a Gorlok statue on the home campus by November 2015 in honor of Webster's Centennial year.

1992 UNIVERSITY CENTER

"The architectural design of the new University Center is splendid. It is a brilliant building that greatly enhances Webster University's campus and improves the quality of life for our students, faculty, and staff."

~ President Daniel H. Perlman

A place to play. A place to exercise. A place to work. A place to meet. A place to relax. A place to do all of these things in one location did not exist until the University Center opened on Webster University's home campus in 1992.

It's hard to imagine life at Webster without the University Center. But that was the case for much of the school's first seventy-five years. During those years, Webster had a number of smaller venues, including the original gym nicknamed the Idle Hour, a shared gym with neighboring Nerinx Hall, and leased space for student activities and athletics in what was called the Plymouth Building. But students had no large gathering place, and Webster's teams played off-campus at various rented facilities after intercollegiate sports began in 1984.

The $5.5 million facility immediately provided sorely needed accommodations for athletic teams, plus casual dining, conference

rooms, workout facilities, a swimming pool, administrative offices, and student activities spaces. Known as "the living room of the university," the center also is enjoyed by alumni and community members, who have access via memberships to the pool and fitness center.

1998 WOMEN'S SOFTBALL BECOMES FIRST WEBSTER TEAM TO QUALIFY FOR NCAA TOURNAMENT

"We were all so new, we were in it together. There wasn't any friction. . . . It was really nice to come together as one team."

~ Pitcher Jeanne (Zes) Gilbert

Webster University's softball team could hardly be termed a candidate for success in 1998. The year before, the first for Webster softball, the team won just six games.

But new talent—in particular, pitcher Jeanne (Zes) Gilbert—put the young program on a path that led to the 1998 team's becoming the first in Webster University history to qualify for the NCAA playoffs in any sport. With Zes, a transfer student, winning fourteen games and striking out eighty while walking only fourteen, Webster posted a 30-5 record, won the St. Louis Intercollegiate Athletic Conference (SLIAC)

championship and advanced to the NCAA playoffs.

Leading contributors included Tara Horn, who hit .495, the highest single-season batting average in Webster softball history. Katie Maynard batted .444, and pitcher Heather Kristof posted eight shutouts while compiling a 10-3 record.

Although they lost their only NCAA playoff game that season, Webster's softball players and Coach Craig Walston had established a dynasty that would go on to win five SLIAC titles and 170 games, while losing just 39 from 1998-2002.

"The athletic program adds to the culture of Webster and lends a vibrancy to the co-curricular community."

~ *Webster University Athletic Director, 1994-2013, Tom Hart*

When Tom Hart became Webster University's men's basketball coach in 1991, he joined a seven-year-old athletic program trying to establish itself. "Our reputation was one of finishing at the bottom end of the conference we had just joined," he said.

Buoyed by the opening of the University Center in 1992—the first on-campus facility with a gym, locker room, fitness center, and offices—Webster athletics had more to offer to prospective recruits. Within a few years, Webster's Gorloks were doormats no more in the St. Louis Intercollegiate Athletic Conference (SLIAC).

The payoff came in the 1999–2000 academic year. Webster's men's and women's teams won the SLIAC All-Sports Award, given to the member school with the best all-around performance in SLIAC's sports. More importantly, the cumulative grade-point average of Webster's athletes that year was 3.11.

Webster has been SLIAC's most dominant school ever since, winning the All-Sports Award fifteen out of sixteen years from 1999–2000 to 2014–15.[34]

213

2012 WEBSTER UNIVERSITY BASEBALL TEAM REACHES NCAA WORLD SERIES

"This will always have a place in their hearts. The experience and the memories that these guys have, and the friends they have made . . . [are] going to last a long time."

~ Webster University Baseball Coach Bill Kurich[35]

The Gorloks reached the pinnacle of college baseball success in 2012 by becoming the first Webster team in any sport to reach an NCAA national championship tournament. Along the way, they won the St. Louis Intercollegiate Athletic Conference (SLIAC) regular-season title and post-season tournament, then captured the NCAA Millington Regional to advance to the NCAA Division III World Series. The Gorloks went 1-2 in the World Series to finish fifth. As the next three seasons proved, 2012 was no fluke.

The Gorloks reached the World Series and were fifth again in 2013. The 2014 team spent two weeks ranked first in the nation in Division III, winning thirty-seven games. The 2015 squad swept the Waterloo Regional and made Webster's third World Series appearance in

four years. From 2010-2015, the baseball team amassed a 210-70 record and six consecutive SLIAC championships. "All of you came to Webster University for a variety of reasons, a variety of majors, a variety of programs, a variety of career goals," said President Beth Stroble. "But what brought you together in this tremendous team effort was this baseball team, and to have such outstanding results as students and as athletes is no small measure of who you are as individuals and who you are as a team."

> *"Chess is more than just a game. It is . . . a philosophy that teaches the importance of strategy, critical thinking, and sportsmanship that can be applied to all areas of life and is not just limited to the game board."*
>
> ~ *Webster University*
>   *Chess Coach Susan Polgar*

A few years ago, a chess-playing friend told Provost Julian Schuster some exciting news: grandmaster Susan Polgar, the nation's leading collegiate chess coach and one of the world's top women's players, wanted to relocate.

Webster followed up. In 2012, Polgar, her Susan Polgar Institute for Chess Excellence (SPICE), and her two-time national champion chess team moved from Texas Tech University to Webster University. Just like that, Webster's new chess program was number one in the United States. "It's a part of the Webster mission to prepare students for individual excellence and

global citizenship; this initiative perfectly fits in accomplishing both," Schuster said.

The chess team won Webster's first national championship in any sport in 2013 and repeated it in 2014. FIDE, the World Chess Federation, named Polgar its instructor of the year in 2014. In 2015, the chess team won its third straight College Chess Final Four championship. The win set a new record for Coach Susan Polgar as the first coach to lead five consecutive winning teams. "I am proud of the Webster University students who are able to compete on the national stage," said President Beth Stroble. "Chess is

Webster Groves City Council Presentation

a global game and it's fitting that the three-time champions represent a global university."

The Susan Polgar Foundation (SPF) sponsors many events to promote critical thinking in boys and girls across the United States and internationally, including the SPF Girls' Invitational, the first all-girls event approved and sanctioned by the United States Chess Federation in 2003.

Locally, the Webster chess program has become an integral part of the community of Webster Groves. Coach Polgar and several players have worked with teachers and students in the Webster Groves School District on chess skills and how to apply them in the classroom. In 2015, the program relocated to the newly reopened Luhr Building, where it has the space to broaden its offerings for the community, including a summer camp for children and a free chess advisory program to the community. In honor of the team's success and its contributions to the community, The Webster Groves City Council proclaimed April 23, 2015, as "Webster University Chess Team Day."

2013 Girls Invitational

Provost Schuster at SPICE Welcome

1966 REPERTORY THEATRE OF ST. LOUIS

"Repertory is blue-collar as well as white-collar theatre. Everybody comes. . . . To survive as a vital force, we must offer something for everyone."

~ *Repertory Theatre of St. Louis actor Larry Linville* [36]

Sr. Marita Michenfelder and Theatre Impact Staff

In the United States, circa 1960, theatre productions staged and acted by professionals existed outside of New York City usually as traveling companies moving from one city to another.[37]

Webster College changed that.

In tandem with the opening of the Loretto-Hilton Center for the Performing Arts at Webster in 1966, the school founded The Repertory Theatre of St. Louis. "The Rep," as it is usually called, has been giving St. Louisans year-round access to local professional theater ever since.

The Rep also partners with Webster University's Conservatory of Theatre Arts to provide invaluable experience to students. This

partnership predates the start of The Rep by five years. In 1961, the Webster Theatre Department began "Theatre Impact," an annual summer outdoor series at nearby Kirkwood Park with a mix of Webster students and professional actors. "Everybody loved it," said Marita Woodruff, then Sr. Marita Michenfelder and the head of Webster's Theatre Department. "It was on a hillside and (there was) a full house every night."

The popularity of the summer series inspired the construction of the Loretto-Hilton and the formation of The Rep. The original company included five junior members who were Webster students. One of the original professional Rep actors was Larry Linville, who later portrayed Major Frank Burns on the popular television series *M*A*S*H.*[38]

Safe House featuring Will Cobbs and Raina Houston

One Man, Two Guvnors featuring Raymond McAnally and Ruth Pferdehirt

A Midsummer Night's Dream

Attendance lagged and finances suffered during Rep's early years, forcing cancellation of the 1970-71 season. President Leigh Gerdine worked with community leaders to put The Rep back on its feet, allowing it to reopen in 1971 as an independent company. Gerdine, "a visionary in the arts in St. Louis," according to dean of the Leigh Gerdine College of Fine Arts and Loretto-Hilton veteran Peter Sargent, helped preserve The Rep's relationship with Webster's theatre program, a partnership that endures to this day.

From its start as a local summer stock company, The Rep has grown to be one of the nation's leading theatre programs and a popular destination for theatre lovers.

Karen Luebbert
and Elmer Arndt

1969 WEBSTER-EDEN PARTNERSHIP

"This agreement is a winning proposition for both institutions. It will allow Eden and Webster to continue to provide education in keeping with our historic core values, as well as to evolve to reflect changes in our student bodies."

~ *Webster University President Elizabeth (Beth) J. Stroble and Eden Theological Seminary President David Greenhaw, 2009*[39]

The Webster-Eden partnership: a textbook example of two schools working together to benefit their students.

In 1969, a year after Eden Theological Seminary opened its Luhr library across the street from Webster, the schools agreed to share the facility as the Eden-Webster Library. Webster's library moved from the second floor of Webster Hall to the facility, providing students at both schools with enhanced library services and resources. Over the years, the two institutions have developed the joint library system on both campuses to meet the changing needs of their students, faculty, staff, alumni, and members of the general public. In 2003, when the Emerson Library opened on the Webster campus, over 600 students, faculty, staff, alumni, and community members formed a human chain to transfer books from Luhr Library to Emerson Library. Today, joint library facilities include the Emerson Library and the Luhr Reading and Reference Library on the Eden campus.

This decades-long partnership, while begun with the joint library system, quickly expanded to many other important collaborations, including joint academic programs; sharing of dormitory, administrative, and athletic facilities; and creation of innovative programs such as entrepreneurship studies for ministers.

In 2009, the institutions signed a new memo of understanding that included the transfer of 5.5 acres and three buildings—the Wehrli Center, Luhr building, and the "White House"—from Eden to Webster. After successful negotiations and proceedings with the City of Webster Groves, in January 2015 the Luhr building became the new home of the university's Information Technology office, the Susan Polgar Institute of Chess Excellence, and the university's award winning chess team.

Enriching Learning through Community Partnerships

John McVeigh and Joyce El-Khoury in the 2015 production of Tobias Picker's *Emmeline*

"The Opera Theatre of Saint Louis has offered a season that's every bit as satisfying, and almost as extensive, as that of the Washington National Opera — on between one-half and one-third of WNO's budget."

~ Anne Midgette, The Washington Post, 2014 [40]

When opera lovers in St. Louis pondered starting an opera company in the mid-1970s, they found the support they needed at Webster University.

President Leigh Gerdine had a love for the arts and a conviction to help them. Earlier, he had revived the struggling Repertory Theatre of St. Louis, a company of professional actors and Webster theatre students who performed at Webster's Loretto-Hilton Center for the Performing Arts.

Gerdine saw similar possibilities for helping opera in St. Louis and giving Webster's students another avenue to work with professionals. The Opera Theatre of Saint Louis (OTSL) was born in 1975 and produced its first festival in 1976.

OTSL offers ambitious productions of modern and classical opera, all performed in English, during a month-long spring festival. Over the years, the OTSL has given two dozen world and two dozen American premieres in the intimate setting of the Loretto-Hilton Center for the Performing Arts.

In 2006, OTSL opened the Sally S. Levy Opera Center on the home campus of Webster University. This modern facility offers office space for the staff and ample rehearsal space for the performers.

Tai Oney and Tim Mead in *Richard the Lionheart*, 2015

Corinne Winters and Anthony Kalil
in the 2015 production of *La rondine*

Magic Flute, 1980

"I am thrilled to see this example of the power of partnership — one that will strengthen The Muny and provide opportunities for Webster students to excel. It is this kind of creative collaboration that transforms lives and enriches communities."

~ *President Elizabeth (Beth) J. Stroble*

In 2011, Webster University and The Muny forged a fitting partnership: America's oldest and largest outdoor theatre joined with one of America's leading university programs for theatre performance students to develop and train performers and production staff.

The agreement strengthens both partners. Students in Webster's Conservatory of Theatre Arts participate in master classes offered by Muny choreographers and directors and in workshop development projects for future seasons. They may also audition for musicals and apply for internships at The Muny. The Muny benefits from tapping into Webster's talented pool of theatre arts students.

"We are always striving to offer our students the best in training, development, and hands-on experience," said Leigh Gerdine College of Fine Arts dean Peter Sargent. "With the leadership of faculty member Lara Teeter, head of Webster's musical theatre program and a regular star of Muny productions, there are natural opportunities for our students to contribute to the performances on the incredible Muny stage."

The original partnership has led to other cooperative efforts, such as a summer intensive for America's most promising senior and junior high school students. Students accepted into the program rehearse and perform at The Muny and attend college-credit classes led by Webster's conservatory faculty.[41]

2012 OFFICE OF CORPORATE PARTNERSHIPS

The Office of Corporate Partnerships (OCP) builds on Webster University's long history of mutually beneficial relationships with the business world.

Established in 2012 by President Beth Stroble, the OCP connects corporate partners with Webster's five colleges and schools, faculty, staff, students, alumni, and extended campuses. Partnerships lead to the delivery of Webster programs that benefit partners, and to collaborating on solutions to community issues of mutual interest.

The OCP manages partnerships with more than 100 corporations and directs programs such as Corporate Cohorts and Global Leaders in Residence. Corporate Cohorts allows organizations to have employees take Webster University courses together and progress together through degree programs. Global Leaders in Residence hosts thought leaders from various disciplines who spend several days on campuses delivering lectures and meeting with students.

Enriching Learning through Community Partnerships

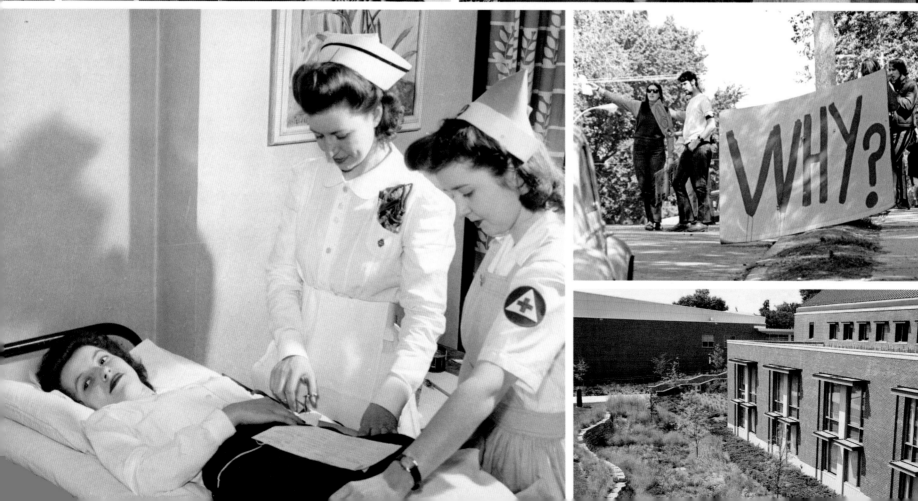

AN ENDURING SPIRIT OF CARING AND INCLUSIVENESS

Since 1915, Webster's mission has been to open doors—doors to a college education first for Catholic women, and later for people with disabilities, minorities, international students, men, disadvantaged youth, veterans and active duty military, working adults, and many others who found a home at Webster. In turn, countless faculty, staff, students, and alumni through the years have reached out to their communities and the university in a variety of ways to provide support, whether it be through financial gifts, volunteering their time and expertise, advocating for justice, or conserving the environment for the next generation. Today, countless people from Webster are making a difference in the lives of communities throughout the world.

Support for Webster's Mission   228

A Commitment to a Diverse and Inclusive University   238

Social Justice and Community Service   250

Environmental Sustainability Yesterday and Today
for the Webster of Tomorrow   262

1928 LORETTO FOUNDATION

"No one, unless he had the courage of a Sister, would have dared to plan an enterprise like this college here, when elsewhere men hesitate to start a college even when they are assured of millions in endowment. The Sisters of Loretto have dared, and they mean their work to go forward."

~ Rev. Daniel Lord, speaking about the Loretto Foundation

Support for Webster's Mission

By the late 1920s, the Sisters of Loretto were teaching in St. Louis parochial schools, operating upper-level academies, and leading a growing college in the St. Louis suburb of Webster Groves (as well as another college in Colorado). The Loretto Foundation was formed to bring together the former students and alumni of all these schools to support the work of the Sisters. The first alumnae reunion was held in September 1929.

One of the foundation's first efforts consisted of raising money for the construction of Webster College's Loretto Hall, a residence hall that would open in September 1928. Various events, including card parties and carnivals, were held to help pay for the $300,000 addition to the college.

In later years, the Loretto Foundation was reorganized to include various college organizations, including the Alumni Association, the Men's Club, and the Women's Club. The Office of Advancement continues the work begun by the Loretto Foundation in raising funds to support the mission of Webster University. Today, the Webster University Alumni Association oversees a number of programs for Webster's more than 176,000 graduates.

2014 Alumni Board

1938

FIRST ENDOWMENT FUND AND FUNDRAISING CAMPAIGNS

"A growing endowment is an integral part of Webster University's ability to carry out our mission."

~ *President Elizabeth (Beth) J. Stroble, 2012*

Webster University's endowment, which reached a record $128.9 million in 2014, started in 1938 with a single donor: Mrs. John C. Corrigan, the mother of a Webster alumna, gave the first contribution.

In subsequent years, foundation grants, generous donors, and fund-raising drives would help the young college weather challenging times and respond to the needs of a changing society.

Perhaps the most critical contributions came following Webster's transition to a secular college in 1967. President Leigh Gerdine sought a single million-dollar donation to help the school move forward. In 1972, the Danforth Foundation responded with a $1.4 million grant. Civic leaders led by General Leif J. Sverdrup and August A. Busch Jr. also engineered a fundraising effort to retire the school's debt, fund programs, provide student aid, and increase the endowment.

Its finances in order, Webster went on to establish campuses in the United States and around the world, and to expand its undergraduate and graduate course offerings. Such growth led to a need for additional facilities and services, and new fundraising campaigns were implemented in response.

The first, from 1985-90, generated $15.3 million for the Sverdrup complex and the University Center. The second major campaign, *New Tradition: For Changing Times, for Changing Lives* (1999-2002), raised $44 million, much of it for the new Emerson Library, Garden Park Plaza garage, and Webster Village apartments.

The university also received $1.16 million as part of a congressional appropriations bill signed by President George W. Bush, the first time the university has been included in such legislation. A U.S. Department of Education Title III

Garden Avenue Donor Plaza

Strengthening Institutions grant of $1.75 million allowed Webster to fund library technology and establish the Faculty Development Center.

The most recent campaign, *Webster Works*, provided a school-record $56 million from 2003-2010. At the closing celebration, President Stroble thanked the donors—all 12,015 of them—and noted the major accomplishments of the campaign, which addressed three key areas: new classroom facilities, increased endowed scholarships and professorships for future students, and current operating needs through the Annual Fund. The campaign created forty-five new scholarships, made possible the East Academic Building and a future interdisciplinary sciences building, and saw faculty/staff participation in the Annual Fund increase from twenty-one percent in 2007-08 to fifty-eight percent in 2010-11.

Jerry Ritter with President Stroble and Provost Schuster

Brenda Newberry, Mark Burkhart, President Stroble, and Ambassador Walker

President Stroble and Marianne Knaup

Jean Hobler

Laurance and Jinny Browning

Ronald and Jan Greenberg

Marilyn Fox

Bruce and Jane Robert with President Stroble

"As committed friends of the university, you, as members of the Daniel Webster Society, have always believed in and supported Webster's expansive horizon and our potential growth in St. Louis and beyond."

~ President Elizabeth (Beth) J. Stroble, 2010

Conseulo Gallagher

For almost thirty years, members of the Daniel Webster Society have proven to be some of the most committed and loyal supporters of Webster University.

Established in 1986, the society recognizes donors making significant gifts. Donors also can establish Daniel Webster Society Annual Scholarships in their names, or in the name of someone they wish to honor.

Today, the society has over 300 members, the most in the organization's history. The society's annual Visionary Award, first given in 2008 to lifetime trustee and former board chairman Laurance Browning and his wife, Jinny, recognizes members who demonstrate unwavering commitment to Webster University. Past Visionary Award winners include Ambassador George Herbert Walker III, Marianne and Warren Knaup, Conseulo Gallagher, Marilyn Fox, Jan and Ronald Greenberg, Jane and Bruce Robert, and Jean Hobler.

The Daniel Webster Society continues the mission of current and past support organizations such as the Alumni Association, Webster College Women's Club (1932), Men's Club (1936), Webster College Community Associates (1968), and Women of Webster (1972). The society complements the many other giving opportunities at Webster, all of which help make it possible to continue the university's mission.

Support for Webster's Mission

2007 ANNUAL SCHOLARSHIP PROGRAM

"It was important to me to keep Kevin's spirit alive. We wanted to focus on the things that Kevin valued, with his Webster education being one of them."

~ *Greg Hunt, father of the late Kevin Hunt (Class of 2002)*

Greg and Cheryl Hunt found a fitting way to honor their late son and Webster University graduate, Kevin: They took advantage of Webster's annual scholarship program to establish a Daniel Webster Society Scholarship in Kevin's name.

The Hunts are two of the many donors who have helped Webster University students by giving to the annual scholarship program, begun in 2007. Nearly 100 students who might not otherwise have the means to attend Webster University benefit annually from the scholarship program. "I'm among the first generation of my family to attend college, and I wouldn't have been able to

do that without scholarship support," said Gabe Bullard, a 2007 Webster graduate who majored in journalism.

"It is our hope that our scholarship support opens doors and allows these students experiences that they don't even imagine at this point," said Marianne Gleich, class of 1966, who has established several Webster University scholarships.

The annual scholarship program is part of a wide array of scholarships, grants, and work study opportunities for Webster students.

Marilyn and Sam Fox with scholarship recipients

President Stroble with scholarship recipients

2012 WEBSTER UNIVERSITY PUBLIC ART COUNCIL

"It's an interesting idea to put works of art in places for people to see and interpret, where it's part of life without being in a museum. Students should take for granted that there are wonderful things here on campus."

~ *Tom Lang, Chair of Webster University's Department of Art, Design and Art History* [42]

More than 1,000 pieces comprise Webster University's collection of art, much of it donated by generous faculty, students, alumni, and other benefactors. The management of this collection, including the installation and display of art works at Webster campuses, is the work of the Webster University Public Art Council, established by President Beth Stroble in 2012.

Led by Provost Julian Schuster, the council recommends display of public art—art on Webster's campuses that appears outside of studios, classrooms, museums, and galleries. Students, faculty, staff, and community art representatives serve on the council.

Webster University's long-standing art initiative owes a great deal to Tom Lang, chair of Webster's Department of Art, Design and Art History and a professor at Webster since 1972. The relationships he developed in the art world over the years have led to many donations, including those by Jan and Ronald Greenberg, who have donated more than 150 works to the university. The Daniel Webster Society honored the Greenbergs' extraordinary support of Webster University with the society's Visionary Award in 2013.

Other pieces came to the university through partnerships such as one with Laumeier Sculpture Park, which loaned the university the eight-foot-tall bronze sculpture, *Window 1/3*, by American artist Jene Highstein, in 2012.

The university is an active partner in several community public art initiatives, including the summer Art & Air festival and the fall Webster Groves Art Walk. A university art museum will be featured in the new Gateway Campus in downtown St. Louis to showcase the university's extensive art collection as well as special art exhibits.

Support for Webster's Mission

1919 TWO FRENCH STUDENTS ENROLL

Marcelle Prévost

"As Loretto College, we were first a college of Catholic women west of the Mississippi, one of the first to reach a population not commonly served in 1915. From that beginning, the founding Sisters of Loretto soon answered a question that became fundamental to our identity — shall we admit international students? The answer was yes."

~ President Elizabeth (Beth) J. Stroble, 2010

The year was 1919, and Loretto College decided to swim against the tide of isolationism that began to rise in the United States after World War I.

Just a year after the war ended, and four years after the founding of the college, the college enrolled its first international students. The students, both from France, were able to receive funding for college under a program sponsored by the French government and US educators.

One of the students, Marcelle Prévost, played a role in the early days of the college. As a student, Prévost contributed poetry and essays to the *Lorettine*, a literary magazine published by the college. After finishing her degree, Prévost completed a master's degree at the Sorbonne in Paris and came back to Webster College to teach French for a number of years.

Prévost's contributions marked the first fruits of Webster University's longstanding commitments to inclusiveness and diversity.

1939

GENEVIEVE HOGAN BECOMES FIRST STUDENT WHO IS BLIND TO GRADUATE FROM WEBSTER

"Webster University's commitment to diversity and inclusion is expressed in many ways, including the vibrant nature of our global community of faculty, staff, and students; the content and focus of our academic programs; and the design of facilities and services. We are honored to receive recognition for initiatives that increase accessibility for those who work and study at Webster."

~ *President Elizabeth (Beth) J. Stroble, 2013*

Genevieve Hogan

Webster University's emphasis on accessibility for those with disabilities has been recognized in recent years by advocates such as Paraquad. But that emphasis was apparent more than seventy-five years ago when Genevieve Hogan enrolled at Webster.

In 1939, Hogan became Webster's first student who was blind to graduate. Some fifty years before the Americans with Disabilities Act required public places to accommodate individuals with disabilities, Webster helped Hogan toward her bachelor's degree in English and French with specialized materials not found at most colleges. Webster was the first local college to provide Braille books for students and to offer a section of Braille books in a school library.

Webster's tradition of inclusiveness continues with a variety of services for individuals with disabilities. These include alternative-format textbooks and assistive technology to help students such as Julie McGinnity succeed. McGinnity, who has been blind since birth, graduated from Webster with honors in 2013 with bachelor's degrees in music and German, and credited much of her success to learning how to read music in Braille while at Webster.

1950 FIRST AFRICAN AMERICAN GRADUATE

Janet Irene Thomas

". . . admit any qualified Catholic student, irrespective of color. . . . When an explanation is asked, simply state that the pupil is Catholic and qualified to meet the high standards of the school . . ."
~ *Joseph E. Ritter, Archbishop of St. Louis, writing to the superior of Webster College, 1947* [43]

Janet Irene Thomas, Webster's first African American graduate, met and exceeded those high standards. An accomplished pianist and vocalist, Thomas overcame many obstacles to break the color line at Webster. After graduation, she continued to be active in the civil rights movement.

Webster's desegregation efforts hit a number of obstacles in the years preceding Thomas's admittance. During a time when segregation of public schools was mandated by Missouri state law, Webster College, then a Catholic school, sought to become the first private college in the state to enroll an African American, in 1943. Despite support from several Catholic clergy and President George Donovan, Mary Aloyse Foster, an African American graduate of a Catholic high school in St. Louis, was denied entrance to Webster by the local Catholic diocese.[44] It wasn't until Joseph E. Ritter became Archbishop of St. Louis in 1946 that Webster College could proceed to admit its first African American students.

Webster has made great strides since those turbulent years and today is recognized for its efforts to provide higher education to a diverse and inclusive student body.

1962 **FIRST MALE STUDENTS**

Webster had been a college for women for forty-seven years before the first male student set foot on campus in 1962. Initially males were only allowed to take courses in art, music, and theatre. The remaining courses (e.g., general education) had to be taken at another school, usually St. Louis University. In 1964, men majoring in fine arts were allowed to take all of their courses at Webster.

The administration continued to gradually open the door to coeducation and by 1967, male enrollment had reached eighty-one. The Board of Directors gave approval for Webster to accept male students in all areas of study starting with the 1968-69 academic year, although Webster did not advertise itself as a fully coed college until 1969. By that time, Webster's board realized that more male students could reverse declining enrollment.

The transition to a coed college was awkward at times. One male student, Jim Ryan, recalled receiving an invitation to an all-campus event "telling me to wear my heels." Nevertheless, Ryan and classmate Dan Coughlin became Webster's first male graduates in 1964.

Daniel Coughlin in study group

Commitment to a Diverse and Inclusive University

1990 SUPPORT FOR AMERICANS WITH DISABILITIES ACT

"We're trying to enhance the integration of people with disabilities into the mainstream of the university so they feel as much a part of Webster as anyone else, because it's their university, too."

~ *Director of the Academic Support Center Karin Niemeyer*

Not long after the Americans with Disabilities Act became law in July 1990, Webster University reinforced its longstanding commitment to accessibility for individuals with disabilities.

In November 1990, Webster held "Differently-Abled Awareness Day" to raise awareness of the challenges faced by individuals with disabilities. Participants, including President Daniel Perlman, negotiated an obstacle course in wheelchairs. Others were blindfolded to experience life without sight. A support dog demonstrated how it had been trained to help individuals with disabilities.

The event illustrated Webster's concern for providing access to higher education for individuals with disabilities, a concern which dates back to the early years of the college. In the

1930s, Webster was the only local college with textbooks and a library section in Braille. That tradition of inclusiveness carries on thanks to the leadership of the Academic Resource Center, which provides services and resources that help students with visual, hearing, mobility, and other disabilities to succeed in their classes. In addition, a campus-wide Accessibility Committee has worked to equip Webster's campuses with accommodations such as automatic doors, wheelchair ramps, and restrooms and on-campus residences that are accessible for individuals with disabilities.

Webster's commitment to individuals with disabilities has been recognized by advocates such as Paraquad, whose St. Louis chapter honored Webster in 2013 for its accessibility for individuals with disabilities.

1991 WEBSTER RECOGNIZED AS ONE OF TOP DEGREE PRODUCERS FOR DIVERSE STUDENTS

"Webster University was founded on the principles of inclusion, and almost 100 years later, we remain committed to this core value."

~ *Associate Vice President of Diversity & Inclusion and Community Engagement Nicole Roach, 2014*

While it's easy to claim a commitment to a diverse and inclusive university, it's a lot harder to back up that claim with hard facts. Webster University has been able to do so and has been recognized for its efforts.

In 1991, *Diverse Issues in Higher Education* (DIHE), a news magazine on diversity in American higher education, began an annual ranking of schools by the number of degrees awarded to students of color. The rankings continue today.

DIHE has ranked Webster highly every year since the very start. The 2014 issue listed Webster first in graduate degree-seeking students of diverse backgrounds among all traditional, private non-profit US schools and public universities.

"Webster's vision of inclusive excellence is based on the premise that excellence is not truly possible without inclusion," noted Provost Julian Schuster. The DIHE's 2014 report found that Webster's already-strong commitment to diversity increased over the previous year. Using data from the U.S. Department of Education for degrees awarded to US citizens, the report found that forty-seven percent of master's degrees conferred by Webster went to African Americans, Asian Americans, Hispanic Americans, and Native Americans, representing a seventeen percent rise over the previous year.

1998

OUTDOOR INTERNATIONAL FLAG DISPLAY ON HOME CAMPUS

With campuses on three continents and students from around the world, Webster had established itself as a global university by the mid-1990s.

President Richard Meyers hit upon a visual demonstration of Webster's worldwide reach: displays of flags from nations represented by Webster's students. Flags from all the home countries of Webster's students went on the rafters in the University Center in 1996, soon joined by smaller flags in the Maria Hall cafeteria and in the foyer before the Winifred Moore Auditorium.

The most eye-catching were the twenty raised in 1998 along the circular drive fronting Webster Hall, built in 1916. Trustee Emerita Margie May donated the flagpoles, which displayed flags of the six countries with Webster campuses and the fourteen nations with the largest numbers of Webster's students. A twenty-first pole was erected in a special space created on the Webster Hall lawn in 2014 to display Webster's Centennial flag.

MULTICULTURAL CENTER AND INTERNATIONAL STUDENT AFFAIRS

The Multicultural Center and International Student Affairs' (MCISA) wide-ranging mission is to create a community that recognizes social differences, respects cultural uniqueness, and facilitates cross-cultural interaction, learning, and appreciation. This mission translates into a cornucopia of endeavors such as an annual international festival where Webster students can sample cultural cuisine, dance, and music, and attend sessions led by internationally known speakers on diversity and inclusiveness. In addition, the center provides a wide range of services and resources for incoming and current international students.

The MCISA evolved in the mid-1990s from what had begun as the Association of Black Collegians a decade earlier. The organization broadened its services to all students of color when it was renamed Minority Affairs in 1992. Reflecting Webster University's global reach, the name was changed to Multicultural Affairs a few years later, then became today's MCISA in 1999.

"One of our primary services is providing students with the tools they need to be successful at Webster University and to work in diverse communities once they graduate."

~ Associate Dean of Students and Director of the Multicultural Center and International Student Affairs Colette Cummings

Commitment to a Diverse and Inclusive University

Commitment to a Diverse and Inclusive University

"Webster University has been a partner and loyal supporter of the Diversity Awareness Partnership since its inception in 2001 and has directly made possible countless effective programs and initiatives."

~ *Diversity Awareness Partnership Executive Director Reena Hajat Carrol* [45]

It's no wonder that Webster University and the Diversity Awareness Partnership (DAP) in St. Louis are almost inseparable. Webster's commitment to a diverse and inclusive university perfectly matches the mission of DAP.

Just as Webster emphasizes diversity at its global campuses, DAP promotes diversity in race, religion, disability, sexual orientation, and gender identity in the St. Louis region.[46] Webster partnered with DAP from its start in 2001 and remains one of the strongest supporters of DAP's work in diversity training, forums, and related programs.[47]

That support took tangible form when Webster opened its Old Post Office campus in 2006. Part

Uppity Theatre Company performance

of the campus was devoted to the office for DAP, and it remains DAP's headquarters to this day.

An important element of Webster's partnership with DAP is Webster's sponsorship of DAP's annual Diversity Summit. The summit is an opportunity for organizations and individuals to share best practices and discuss action steps to improve inclusiveness in the St. Louis area.

2011 TRANSITIONS ACADEMIC PREP (TAP) PROGRAM

"I am very proud that my son attended this life-changing program. He left TAP with a new vision, a sense of self, and the confidence to succeed at Webster University."

~ *TAP parent, 2014*

The transition to college life has never been easy. But with research showing stress levels rising in recent years among college freshmen,[48] Webster University did something to ease the path of new students with records that indicate they might face academic challenges.

Erin Bullerdieck and the Academic Resource Center proposed the Transitions Academic Prep (TAP) program in 2011, and it began that year. The free program welcomes twenty-five conditionally-admitted students to a weeklong session at the St. Louis campus each summer. Participants live on campus and develop friendships with other new students.

Through one-on-one coaching and workshops, students learn writing and research skills, how to manage stress in and out of the classroom, strategies to succeed as a college student, and effective communication skills. Those who pass the course receive one university credit.

Weekly one-on-one meetings between TAP students and their academic counselors continue throughout their first semester, helping to assure that students successfully employ the skills that they have learned.

Before TAP was established at Webster, the difference in retention rates for conditionally admitted students and those admitted without conditions hovered at six percent; since Transitions, that retention gap has narrowed to one percent. Transitions has had a significant impact on the success of program participants, helping them stay in school and remain engaged academically.

Commitment to a Diverse and Inclusive University

Nicole Roach

"Diversity is about a frame of mind. It's about the ability to connect and communicate with people from all backgrounds . . . no matter their color, race, sex, age, sexual orientation, abilities, or socioeconomic background."

~ Associate Vice President of Diversity & Inclusion and Community Engagement Nicole Roach

At a Delegates' Agenda in the fall of 2012, Webster University students and President Beth Stroble began a dialog on diversity and inclusion, which has been a priority of President Stroble's for many years.

She had established a diversity and inclusion office at the University of Akron and appointed Lee Gill as Akron's chief diversity officer. In February 2013, Webster held its first Global Inclusion and Diversity Summit, with Lee Gill as the keynote speaker.

Shortly afterward, President Stroble established the Office of Diversity & Inclusion and Community Engagement at Webster. Nicole Roach, a Webster graduate, director of the Old Post Office Campus, and a recognized leader on workplace diversity, was appointed to head the new office.

Following up on those actions, and on recommendations from the working group on diversity and inclusion, President Stroble appointed a Diversity Council in 2014. The twenty-one-member council advises senior administration and academic and administrative units to ensure that Webster's internal and external relationships and business partnerships reflect Webster's commitment to diversity and inclusion.

2013 SUGGS SCHOLARSHIP

Olivia Perez will never forget the phone call in 2013. While shopping with her family, she heard she had won the first Webster University Dr. Donald M. Suggs Scholarship.

"We were just jumping up and down in the store crying," Perez said. "It felt like the biggest blessing I could have asked for." Perez, a media communications major, hopes to work in the entertainment industry. In addition, she wants to give back to the communities in which she lives by "helping young people figure out what they want their paths in life to be," just as she was helped in choosing her stellar path by her parents, by Dr. Suggs, and by Webster.

Nicole Roach, President Stroble, and Provost Schuster with Olivia Perez

President Beth Stroble established the scholarship and named it for former Webster University trustee Dr. Donald M. Suggs, a St. Louis oral surgeon and publisher of the *St. Louis American* newspaper. "Dr. Suggs is a respected leader who has advocated for people, policies, and practices that enhance opportunity, facilitate inclusion, and eliminate inequities," she said. "Webster University is honored to make this tangible commitment to education in Dr. Suggs' name." The scholarship awards up to $100,000 over four years. Designed to recruit and retain top students who are underrepresented in higher education, the Suggs Scholarship is the largest of six in Dr. Suggs' name at Missouri universities. Joshua Tyler received the second Suggs Scholarship in 2014.

Commitment to a Diverse and Inclusive University

Social Justice and Community Service

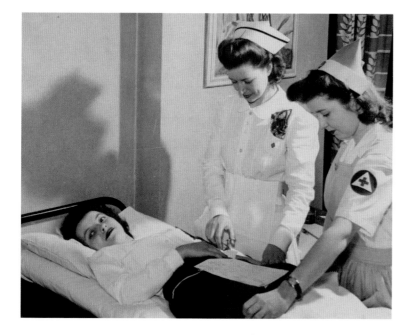

"Each year Webster University collects on average 100 units of blood. Considering each unit can save up to three lives every year, Webster students, faculty, and staff potentially help 300 hospital patients in their community."

~ *Terry Deters, Mississippi Valley Regional Blood Center, 2015*

With World War II raging and the need for blood acute, Webster stepped up and became the first St. Louis college to establish a blood bank.

The concept of a blood bank was relatively new. Established earlier in the war, the process required medical personnel to collect, preserve, and store blood so it could be ready to be shipped when needed by the sick and wounded.[49]

Webster College embraced the idea, and a drive chaired by senior Margaret Robinson established the blood bank. The effort collected about 140 pints of blood on February 10, 1944.

Students, faculty, and staff have continued to meet the urgent need for blood through drives held regularly under the sponsorship of the Student Health Services and Counseling & Life Development departments on the St. Louis campus.

1962

WEBSTER STUDENTS PARTICIPATE IN CIVIL RIGHTS SIT-IN

"It's one thing to hear about the sit-ins and demonstrations in the South; somehow, it's easy to casually watch newsfilms of picket lines. But it's quite another thing to actually participate in a demonstration yourself. It's a little sobering but at the same time, you feel like you're doing something to help."

~ *Webster student newspaper, May 4, 1962*

As the social issues of the 1960s heated up, so did the activism of Webster students, faculty, and administration. A prime example occurred in 1962, when Webster students joined a sit-in at a local restaurant that refused to serve African Americans.

Student activism took other forms. In 1962, the student body of Webster College wrote letters supporting James Meredith's attempt to attend the all-white University of Mississippi.

Many faculty were also active in the civil rights movement. Sr. Barbara Ann Barbato memorably demonstrated in her nun's habit at the Democratic Convention in Chicago in 1968. Sr. Anna Barbara Brady—who later married fellow Webster professor Ed Sakurai—participated, along with Barbato and Webster students, in the antiwar March on Washington in 1969.

Today, student activism in civil rights is manifested in many ways, from inviting civil rights activists to speak on campus to protests related to recent events in Ferguson, Missouri. in 2015, Webster students joined college students from around the country in Ferguson Alternative Spring break, a project designed to strengthen and rebuild the Ferguson community through projects including voter registration, community beautification, and tutoring.[50]

Webster community rally in support of Ferguson

"From our children I am learning to see, to view the ordinary with their beautiful gift of wonder . . . For all they have granted me I can only hope to return the less exciting basics of the alphabet, numbers, art, and music. How little that is! I thank Webster College for giving me this opportunity to learn—I shall never have another like it."

~ *Suzanne Doyle, Webster sabbatical student, July 16, 1965*

Motivated by issues such as civil rights and urban poverty, Webster students and faculty brought love, compassion, and education to those in need.

In January 1965, the Webster-Mullanphy Center opened near Pruitt-Igoe, a collection of high-rise public housing buildings on the northwestern edge of downtown St. Louis.[51] Located in an area rife with poverty and crime,[52] the center presented an opportunity to address those issues through education. After relocating to a larger building, Webster operated a preschool near the center.

Members of the Loretto Community and Webster faculty staffed the center. Webster students taught and lived there, some as part of their sabbatical semester, which gave them the opportunity for off-campus learning experiences under close supervision. More importantly, the residents were able to reach out and provide support through tutoring programs, connecting those in need to available resources, holding community meetings, and just being caring neighbors.

We knew . . . "that we were not only bringing good to the people with whom we worked but that they were pouring out their goodness, and their faith and confidence and trust in us" wrote Sr. Ann Christopher Delich in an undated letter to the Webster faculty.

"Upward Bound made me think . . . I had always had trouble with math, but my teachers in Upward Bound showed me how to see the relationship between things, which is all math is. It was a great help in getting me ready for college. Maybe I can do something like that for somebody else."
~ *Alice McNamee, graduate and junior program assistant for Webster's Upward Bound program* [53]

In the early 1960s, Webster College gained a national reputation for its progressive teacher education curriculum. Sr. Jacqueline Grennan, who helped develop that program, was at the forefront of national trends and served on a variety of federal boards, including the steering committee that created Project Head Start for disadvantaged preschool children.

So it made perfect sense that in 1965, Webster College became one of the first six Pre-College Centers in a companion program called Upward Bound. Upward Bound was designed to help disadvantaged students complete high school and prepare for college through academic instruction, tutoring, counseling, and mentoring. Each year the program offered English and mathematics classes, workshops on a variety of topics, and cultural and recreational activities to about 200 high school students who attended classes on Saturdays during the school year and daily during an eight-week summer session. As of 1970, nearly sixty percent of the participants

had either graduated from or were still enrolled in college. [54]

Due to federal budget cuts, Webster's participation in Upward Bound ended in 1971. Webster University, however, continues to help today's pre-college students through efforts such as the Transitions Academic Prep (TAP) program for incoming freshmen.

1970 STUGENT STRIKE

"By staging a strike within the Webster College Community . . . we are using the freedom given us by an open administration to use the college as a forum for effectively communicating student opinion to the public. In no way are we striking against the college, the administration, or the faculty. All our actions will be non-violent and calculated to encourage intelligent involvement in the vital social issues immediately before us."

~ *Statement from the Webster College Strike Committee*

As the Vietnam War escalated in the late 1960s and early 1970s, so did the anti-war protests on many US campuses. One such protest held at Kent State University on May 4, 1970, ended in tragedy when four students were shot and killed by members of the Ohio National Guard.

Alarmed by what they termed an "emergency situation," a number of concerned Webster faculty and students formed a committee and called for a strike on May 6, 1970. Beyond mourning the Kent State deaths and protesting the broadening of the war, the committee's goal was "to unite in order to work for a sane, reasonable solution to our domestic and foreign problems . . . and to unite in creating a constructive, positive, peaceful method of dissent."

Although classes were not officially cancelled, very few were held that day. Instead, students participated in a number of activities, including sit-ins in administrative offices, passing out leaflets and petitions to the community, an evening assembly of speeches, readings and song, and a benefit performance by the theatre department to raise funds to send to Kent State.

The strike, as well as other anti-war protests and moratorium rallies that were held during those years, reflected the strong convictions on the part of many faculty, staff, and students.

254

1988 HUMAN RIGHTS EDUCATION PROJECT

Art Sandler

Even before the 1993 World Conference of Human Rights called for educational programs in international human rights, Webster was raising awareness of these issues.

Art Sandler, a professor of philosophy, started the Human Rights Education Project (HREP) at Webster in 1988. HREP raised students' awareness of international human rights and was a first step toward today's Institute for Human Rights and Humanitarian Studies at Webster.

In 1996, HREP's work helped establish a certificate in international studies at Webster. Nine years later, Sandler headed the effort that led to Webster's undergraduate degree in human rights, the first in the United States.

Like Sandler, Dr. Roy Tamashiro is another well-respected human rights educator at Webster. A professor of education, Tamashiro has dedicated his life to peace research and activism, including leading study trips to Japan, arranging for an exhibit in 2010 of Hiroshima-Nagasaki A-bomb photographs sponsored by the Hiroshima Peace Culture Foundation (HPCF), and partnering with the HPCF and the Truman Presidential Library to host a live video conference between American scholars and hibakusha—survivors of the bombings. It was on his recommendation and that of student Tammy Mueller that Webster University conferred an honorary doctorate degree on Hiroshima atom bomb survivor Koko Tanimoto Kondo and invited her to speak at Webster's 2014 commencement.[55]

Roy Tamashiro and Koko Tanimoto Kondo

1989

WEBSTER STARTS MONTHLY DINNERS FOR THE HOMELESS

Social Justice and Community Service

"I feel so blessed in my own life. I have so much and I see people who have so little. It is a privilege to help another human being, to serve someone a hot meal. It doesn't change their life, but it makes it a little better."

~ Anna Barbara Sakurai

Anna Barbara Sakurai

Webster University professor Anna Barbara Sakurai (formerly Sr. Anna Barbara Brady) took action on issues that mattered. Whether it was helping students of all ages to understand math, developing new ways to enrich undergraduate education, or planning and demonstrating for peace, Sakurai refused to sit on the sidelines.

In that spirit, she and her husband, Ed Sakurai, also a Webster professor, led volunteers in giving a monthly fried chicken dinner for the homeless at Sts. Peter and Paul Church in the Soulard neighborhood of St. Louis in 1989. Webster University's dinners for the homeless have continued ever since and are part of the daily meals program offered by Peter and Paul Community Services. Dedicated Webster volunteers spend about three hours each month preparing and serving meals, then cleaning up.

The Sakurais headed the Webster dinners for many years. Anna Barbara Sakurai, a faculty member for forty years, passed away in 2011. "She never said, 'Somebody ought to do something.' She was soft-spoken, but she had a real strength behind that," said Tom Burnham, director of the St. Peter and Paul Center.

Drs. Mary Ann Drake and Anne Schappe, professors of nursing, lead the Webster dinners for the homeless today.

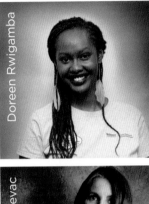

Doreen Rwigamba

Semra Ramosevac

Julienne Uwingabire

"Making a gift of learning available to someone who might not have lived if she had stayed in her own country should serve as a growing beacon of peace and hope from the first-ever truly international university."

~ *President Richard S. Meyers*

Richard Meyers became president of Webster University toward the end of the war in Bosnia. He wanted to find a way to reach out to young people whose studies had been disrupted by the conflict.

In 1995, Meyers established the Presidential International Refugee Scholarship. That first award went to Semra Ramosevac, who had come to the United States from Sarajevo, a city besieged from 1992-1995 during the Bosnian War. Ramosevac graduated in 1997 with a major in biology and a minor in Spanish. "I have enjoyed Webster every day," she said after graduation. Today, she is a public health professional with the Centers for Disease Control and Prevention in Atlanta.

Another successful student, Sara Sabaa, came to Webster in 2008 from Iraq and Syria with the support of President Meyers, associate vice-president Deborah Dey, and faculty member Anna Barbara Sakurai. She was able to complete her studies with tuition provided by the university and housing provided by the Sisters of Loretto at the nearby Loretto Center.

Today, following in their footsteps are three current Rwandan students on full scholarships established by President Beth Stroble in 2011 in partnership with the Dr. Lawrence J. Jehling family, who had enabled Rwandan refugees and cousins Olive Mukabalisa and John Munyarugamba to attend and graduate from Webster University. Doreen Rwigamba, Josiane Umuyhoza, and Julienne Uwingabire entered Webster as freshmen in 2012 and will graduate in 2016.

Social Justice and Community Service

257

1995 WEBSTER WORKS WORLDWIDE

"Community service makes you feel really good about yourself. I think that's the biggest part of community service for me . . . It's a really great feeling to know that you have helped somebody out in their time of need."

~ Nick Dunne (Class of 2011)

Webster's students, faculty, staff, and alumni have devoted immeasurable time and resources to community service since the college opened in 1915. Nothing exemplifies this spirit of giving better than Webster Works Worldwide, an annual day of service begun in 1995.

Held each October at all of Webster's worldwide locations, the event succeeds because it is community-based and volunteer-driven and builds long-term relationships within communities.

Led by a team of dedicated events staff, volunteers organize their own teams, select organizations or people they wish to help, and coordinate their activities. Visiting daycare and senior centers, planting gardens, building homes, knitting warm clothing for the underserved, sorting canned goods at food pantries, cleaning, painting, raking—Webster Works Worldwide volunteers do what is needed to make their communities better places.

Founded by President Richard Meyers in 1995, Webster Works Worldwide has grown every year and has enlisted more than 30,000 volunteers who have logged more than 128,000 hours of service.

1996 GENEVA CAMPUS LAUNCHES ANNUAL HUMANITARIAN CONFERENCE

"The tradition of the International Humanitarian Conference at Webster University Geneva began in 1996 with the support of the United Nations High Commissioner for Refugees, the International Committee of the Red Cross, and the Geneva authorities. Every year, the conference welcomes academics, practitioners, decision makers, and students to address a topical humanitarian issue. For the 20th conference, I had the honor of being a part of the organizing committee, and I would encourage any student to get involved in such a high-profile learning and networking experience."

~ *Tenzin Loeden Bhugyal, Webster student volunteer at the 2015 International Humanitarian Conference*

From an idea for a one-time event involving a single campus, Webster University's International Humanitarian Conference has become an annual gathering of leading humanitarian experts from around the world as well as representatives from Webster's home campus and worldwide network.

The Humanitarian Conference presents a unique learning experience for Webster's students at the Geneva campus. In addition to listening to humanitarian leaders, the students play an active role in running the event. It is an audacious undertaking, involving about forty speakers and as many as 400 visitors over two days. Each year's conference has a single theme, such as "Family, Migration and Separation" in 2015.

First held in 1996 as a local undertaking by the Geneva campus, the conference has grown to encompass all of Webster University under the auspices of the College of Arts & Sciences' Institute of Human Rights and Humanitarian Studies. The conference's location has remained in the canton of Geneva, home to many international organizations.

2008 INSTITUTE FOR HUMAN RIGHTS AND HUMANITARIAN STUDIES

Ishmael Beah

Year of International

HUMAN RIGHTS

College of Arts & Sciences

Webster University
2008-09

Celebrating the 60th anniversary
of the United Nations'
Universal Declaration of Human Rights

"Human rights education repositions students as members of a global community instead of simply as national citizens."

~ *Lindsey Kingston, Director, Institute for Human Rights and Humanitarian Studies* [56]

A key element in accomplishing Webster University's mission to "transform students for global citizenship and individual excellence" is the College of Arts & Sciences' Institute for Human Rights and Humanitarian Studies.

Established in 2008, the institute fosters global citizenship through a variety of programs and activities. These include opportunities for students to earn an undergraduate major, minor or certificate, or a graduate degree, in international human rights. Students can intern or volunteer with non-governmental organizations worldwide, and can publish research in Webster's *Righting Wrongs: A Journal of Human Rights.* Faculty members research issues such as genocide, statelessness, human trafficking, and disability rights.

The institute heightens awareness of global issues through the Year of International Human Rights (YIHR). Observed since 2008, the sixtieth anniversary of the Universal Declaration of Human Rights, YIHR features guest lectures, a film series, art performances, and reading programs. The first guest lecturer was Sierra Leonean author and human rights activist Ishmael Beah. Each YIHR concludes with the Human Rights Conference, a two-day event on the St. Louis campus featuring lectures and discussions focused on a central theme. Themes of past conferences included rights of the family, disability rights, rights of indigenous and stateless peoples, refugee and migrant rights, and women's rights.

"Rally on Front Lawn— Where Do We Go From Here?"

~ *Title of concluding event at first Earth Day observance at Webster, 1970*

Environmental Sustainability

Today's sustainability movement owes much to the first Earth Day on April 22, 1970. An estimated twenty million Americans took part in a national teach-in on environmental issues and protests against pollution.[57]

At Webster College, participants gathered for a program jointly sponsored by Webster and neighboring Eden Theological Seminary. Speakers included two still connected with Webster as emeritus professors: Dr. Phil Sultz presented "The Subtle World," and Dr. Fred Stopsky spoke on "Politics or Change." Activities concluded with a rally on the front lawn.

That first Earth Day ignited a spirit of activism in environmental issues, manifested in student-led activities at Webster such as a recycling program in 1973. Webster University has celebrated Earth Day and Earth Month annually with festivals and ecological demonstrations. Most recently, in 2014, the Department of Dance planned a National Water Dance at the home campus in conjunction with similar events at seventy institutions in thirty states to promote water sustainability.

1990

STUDENTS DRIVE STYROFOAM BAN ON CAMPUS

"We've been very supportive [of the ban], but the most important part is that it was initiated by students and they carried it out."

~ Dean of Student Services Mark Govoni

Noting that cups, trays, and other food service items made of styrofoam require many years to decompose, Webster University students took action in 1990.

Students for Social Action (SSA), a group active on environmental issues at the St. Louis campus, launched a petition asking Webster's administration to ban styrofoam. SSA gathered 270 signatures in just two days from students and faculty. Impressed by the students' initiative in promoting a more sustainable environment, Webster's leadership quickly

agreed and requested that the bookstore and food service phase out the use of items made of styrofoam.

"The administration's support of our efforts to ban styrofoam from campus shows that they are taking the first step toward making the commitment to environmental consciousness," the SSA's Danielle Reamey said at the time. "That's good, because we feel that universities should be the leaders in changing our environmental attitudes."

Environmental Sustainability

Environmental Sustainability

"Sustainability in education is more than recycle bins in classrooms. It's about global citizenship. As educators, we should be helping students analyze what they are doing, where they are going, and how these decisions impact their neighbors locally and globally."

~ *Lori Diefenbacher, Coordinator of Master of Arts and Graduate Certificate programs in Education for Global Sustainability*

As part of Webster University's mission to transform students for global citizenship, Webster established its first curriculum in sustainability in 2009.

Webster initially offered a certificate in education for global sustainability with a goal of providing students with knowledge, skills, and tools to guide schools, organizations, and communities toward global sustainability. In subsequent years, Webster expanded sustainability education to include an undergraduate minor and a certificate, an MA degree in education for global sustainability, and MS and MBA degrees with a sustainability emphasis.

Lori Diefenbacher, a longtime faculty member and leader in sustainability education, brought Webster's sustainability education to a wider audience when Webster held its first Summer Sustainability Institute in 2011 for educators of students in pre-kindergarten through twelfth grade. The annual three-day event at the St. Louis campus features speakers and workshops to help teachers enlighten students to be responsible and take action for a more sustainable environment.

"I don't want to look back and regret not doing anything or taking any kind of action to stop environmentally destructive behaviors."

~ *Sustainability Coordinator Lindsey Lafore, 2015*

Empowering the Webster community to promote environmental responsibility is the mission of the Sustainability Coalition.

Formalized in 2009, the coalition encourages students, faculty, and staff to become members and get involved in sustainability initiatives through discussion and action. The coalition sponsors an annual conference, a quarterly forum to discuss campus and community sustainability issues, and awards $1,000 grants for student-led sustainability projects.

In partnership with Webster Students for Environmental Sustainability, the coalition has helped jump-start a number of sustainability projects on the St. Louis campus. They include a faculty-student proposal to transform a retention pond near Webster Village into a natural habitat and research area. Several environmentally friendly transportation options have also been developed:

- installing new bike racks;

- partnering with Metro Transit since 2012 to offer UPass, a free pass for students, faculty, and staff to ride public transportation;

- providing a hybrid car on campus beginning in 2014 that students can rent through CarShare, a program from Enterprise Holdings Inc.

Environmental Sustainability

"This is a significant advancement for Webster's efforts to become more sustainable. . . . We initially applied for a silver certification, but the reviewers felt that we had exceeded those standards and gave us gold."

~ *Provost, Senior Vice President and Chief Operating Officer Julian Z. Schuster*

Although built with sustainability in mind, the East Academic Building (EAB) has exceeded expectations since it opened in 2012.

The U.S. Green Building Council affirmed this when it certified the EAB for the gold level in Leadership in Energy and Environmental Design (LEED) in 2013. LEED is a nationally recognized certification for the design, construction, and operation of high-performance green buildings.

The gold certification resulted from the EAB's numerous sustainability features. They include an abundance of natural light, thirty-five percent reduction of energy use, proximity to public transportation, and lockers and changing rooms for bicycle riders. A "green roof" containing 22,824 plants in a growing medium over a waterproofing membrane increases energy efficiency.

Sustainability at the EAB includes two rain gardens on the surrounding grounds. The gardens comprise a sustainable alternative for storm water management by filtering contaminants out of rainwater before returning it to groundwater.

2014 WEBSTER GOES SOLAR

"The primary reason that Webster is investing in sustainable infrastructure is to reduce the amount of waste from our locations and to become better stewards of our environment."

~ *Vice President and Chief Financial Officer Greg Gunderson*

The year 2014 saw Webster University tap into the most sustainable energy source around— the sun.

Early in the year, Webster installed what is believed to be the largest solar panel array on a university in St. Louis, mounting seven arrays on six buildings. The panels are expected to save $900,000 in energy costs during the panels' first twenty-five years of operation.

In September 2014, Webster began operating the first EnGo solar kinetic recharging station in the United States. Located outside the East Academic Building, the station can charge up to fourteen mobile devices for free, thanks to energy from solar panels and kinetic charging tiles. The panels cover the station, and the tiles in the ground in front of the station produce electricity every time someone walks on them. The station also provides free WiFi and an emergency phone. A second, portable EnGo station provides "on the go" access in additional areas of the campus. The EnGo stations came to Webster through a partnership with The Volta Group, which was co-founded by Webster alumnus Branko Zivkovic and EnGo co-creator and CEO Petar Mirovic, a Webster doctoral student.

The charging stations and solar panel arrays join an earlier solar energy project on the St. Louis campus. In 2012, Webster installed solar-powered trash and recycling compactors at several locations on campus.

THE FUTURE

Just as the arc of the Earth makes it impossible to see beyond the horizon, so too we can only see a limited distance into the future. Such limitations didn't stop the Sisters of Loretto from having the courage to act 100 years ago and establish a college for women seeking a quality education. With faith and commitment, they guided Webster through uncertain times and left a legacy that continues to inspire to this day. As we turn to the future, today's leaders also face an array of challenges both within an increasingly complex university and externally from a world of exponential change. With the help of its worldwide community, Webster University is combining a global perspective with values of excellence, innovation, and inclusion in a new strategic plan that will guide the university to a brilliant future.

The Centennial Year: Bridge to the Future   270

A Visionary Plan for the Future   275

"This was a year of reflecting upon who we are as a university community, honoring our founders' vision, and celebrating the innovative and resilient faculty, staff, and students who persevered through Webster's first century. Our Centennial celebrations both inspired and engaged the Webster community and the communities in which we serve."

~ *President Elizabeth (Beth) J. Stroble*

The initial public celebration of Webster University's Centennial came with the debut of the official Centennial flag on the home campus on July 17, 2014.

President Beth Stroble; Provost Julian Schuster; and Centennial planning chair, Webster alumna, and former trustee Elizabeth Robb raised the flag in front of Webster Hall, which opened in 1916 as the first building on the St. Louis campus. The flag symbolizes "100 years of students pursuing their dreams, and a testament to the leaders, staff, and, most importantly, the faculty helping our students achieve their goals," said Provost Schuster. Webster University's international campuses hoisted centennial flags later in the year.

Throughout the remainder of 2014 and into 2015, a series of signature events was held to commemorate the Centennial year and to prepare for the launch of Webster's second century, including a Global Student Leaders Summit, a film series, *A Century through Cinema*, and *Illuminate Your Mind Faculty Talks of the Century*.

Among these signature events was the very special 2015 commencement. In this milestone year, 6,574 graduates from 110 countries earned their degrees across the world. This brought the total number of Webster University alumni to over 176,000 for its first 100 years. Centennial year graduates celebrated through commencement ceremonies at Webster campuses on four continents, including the university's largest ceremony held in St. Louis on May 9. The Geneva, Leiden, Thailand, and Vienna campuses were among the campus locations holding local commencement ceremonies that day.

At the main commencement ceremony in St.

L-R: Sr. Barbara Ann Barbato, Dwight Bitikofer, Helen Hagen, and Sanford Zimmerman

Jenifer Lewis

Gwyneth Williams

THE CENTENNIAL YEAR: BRIDGE TO THE FUTURE

Louis, held at the historic Muny amphitheatre, faculty were led in the processional by Faculty Senate president Dr. Gwyneth Williams, who carried the new mace crafted for the Centennial year. The 2015 commencement speaker, acclaimed actress, singer, and community activist Jenifer Lewis was one of five standouts from Webster's history receiving honorary doctoral degrees to commemorate Webster's 100th year:

- Lewis received the Doctor of Humane Letters for her outstanding stage and screen career and her many international community engagement efforts.

- Sister Barbara Ann Barbato, who joined Webster's faculty in 1963, received the Doctor of Pedagogy for her lifelong work as an educator.

- Dwight Bitikofer, an alumnus from 1978, received the Doctor of Letters for co-founding the *Webster-Kirkwood Times* and for his work as an award-winning journalist.

- Helen Hagen, an alumna with two degrees —one in 1944 and another in 1982—received the Doctor of Humanities for her work as co-founder of St. Louis PBS station, KETC-TV, and her continued work in the community.

- Sanford J. (Sandy) Zimmerman received the Doctor of Laws in recognition of his chairing Webster's first lay board in 1967—a pivotal time in Webster's history—and his continued guidance and generosity toward Webster.

In President Stroble's commencement address, she introduced the full debut of Webster University's new alma mater, "Webster U. You Are Our Home." Stroble spoke of the desire for a new alma mater that represents the university's mission in its second century and congratulated Webster student Christopher Poetz, the winner of the alma mater contest, for his composition. The Webster University Chamber Singers performed the new alma mater along with the graduates and their guests.

Signature Centennial events continued through fall 2015—including the *St. Louis Business Journal*/Webster University 'Stars Come Home' Homecoming; a time capsule installation and dedication; a Centennial concert, *Missouri Verses and Voices* at Powell Symphony Hall; and Centennial grand finale gala and open house events.

2015 A VISIONARY PLAN FOR THE FUTURE

Webster University's first 100 years tell a compelling story, a story of a small Catholic college for women that has grown into a secular, coeducational, global university. Along the way it has pioneered delivering quality education to an increasingly diverse student body, not just throughout the United States but on four continents and via the Internet. From a mid-western school whose first graduating class numbered only two, Webster now has more than 176,000 alumni from over 100 countries.

The year 2015 marks a time for celebrating those achievements and for setting a course to greater accomplishments. "Those who came before us faced enormous challenges and persevered. This university, brilliantly resilient, has always managed to use those circumstances to its advantage to be better in the future. That's what we will need to do now," said President Beth Stroble. "We're going to do that by focusing on what we believe the aim of education to be, not just now, but in the future."

Stroble and the Webster University community foresee capitalizing on Webster's strengths as a technologically connected, globally focused

university to transform students for global citizenship and individual excellence. Doing that requires what Stroble and Provost Julian Schuster call "a new paradigm in the internationalization of higher education."

The paradigm calls for thinking beyond the typical study abroad trips that provide short-term experiences isolated from much of the curriculum at many colleges and universities. Too often, students and teachers are moved from one geographic location to another without the opportunity to broaden and deepen their knowledge of the world.

Webster University, however, has been different. Its international campuses bring together students and faculty from a variety of countries for a truly immersive learning opportunity. Students experience other cultures both in the classroom and through a variety of co-curricular activities while living for an extended period of time in another country.

"Unlike other American universities who have attempted to open satellite campuses in other parts of the world, we are integrating ourselves into the local environment," Schuster says. "Our advisory board for our campus in Vienna, for example, includes Vienna campus alumni who are prominent members of the Viennese community. They perceive Webster University as an American-Austrian university. That is a value proposition that very few other universities have in the world."

Webster's achievements in internationalization are indicative of its historical willingness to embrace change and innovation. Globalization "was such a part of Webster University from its inception that we were ahead of the curve," Stroble said. "Again, we're an institution that prides itself on meeting a need and being entrepreneurial, and naturally we saw opportunities outside of St. Louis well before it became cool to be global." [58]

Simply being global, however, is no longer enough in today's higher educational environment. A truly global university must operate through a network of campuses that mutually enhance each other through sharing of information, knowledge, and resources. The mobility of students, faculty, and staff is enhanced by joint activities across various geographic communities and thus produces impact on a global scale.

A recent example of these kinds of activities was the 2015 Global Student Leadership Summit, which brought together student leaders from the United States and seven international locations to work on a common project. Similarly, the annual Global Leadership Academy hosts a cohort of US and international faculty and staff for year-long professional development while spending time on several Webster campuses. Within the curriculum itself, the Global Citizenship Program, taken by undergraduate students at all of Webster's campuses worldwide, instills a world view and globally relevant skills in Webster's graduates.

Taking all of that into consideration, Stroble and Schuster believe that Webster is a pioneer of the new paradigm in global higher education.

Going forward, Webster's worldwide campuses will connect as centers of educational excellence in one large global system. The blueprint for that interaction can be found in *Global Impact for the*

GLOBAL IMPACT FOR THE NEXT CENTURY

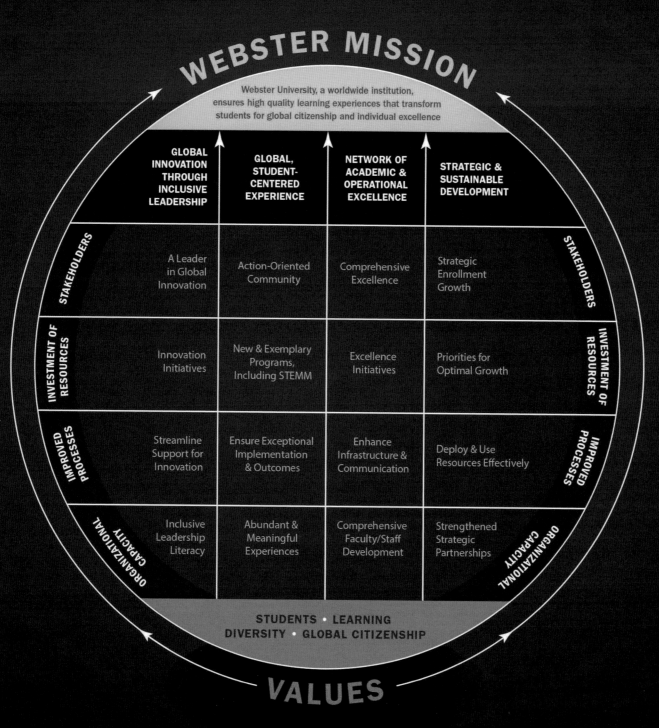

WEBSTER MISSION

Webster University, a worldwide institution, ensures high quality learning experiences that transform students for global citizenship and individual excellence

	GLOBAL INNOVATION THROUGH INCLUSIVE LEADERSHIP	GLOBAL, STUDENT-CENTERED EXPERIENCE	NETWORK OF ACADEMIC & OPERATIONAL EXCELLENCE	STRATEGIC & SUSTAINABLE DEVELOPMENT
STAKEHOLDERS	A Leader in Global Innovation	Action-Oriented Community	Comprehensive Excellence	Strategic Enrollment Growth
INVESTMENT OF RESOURCES	Innovation Initiatives	New & Exemplary Programs, Including STEMM	Excellence Initiatives	Priorities for Optimal Growth
IMPROVED PROCESSES	Streamline Support for Innovation	Ensure Exceptional Implementation & Outcomes	Enhance Infrastructure & Communication	Deploy & Use Resources Effectively
ORGANIZATIONAL CAPACITY	Inclusive Leadership Literacy	Abundant & Meaningful Experiences	Comprehensive Faculty/Staff Development	Strengthened Strategic Partnerships

STUDENTS · LEARNING
DIVERSITY · GLOBAL CITIZENSHIP

VALUES

A VISIONARY PLAN FOR THE FUTURE

Next Century, Webster University's strategic plan for 2015-2020. "With this new strategic plan, we will affirm our heritage of providing quality education where we see need while identifying and advancing strategic directions to ensure Webster thrives into the future," said President Beth Stroble

Vice Provost Nancy Hellerud chaired the strategic planning process, which utilized the input of hundreds of faculty, staff, and students throughout the Webster system. Their thoughtful and diligent work established four themes that map the course of Webster University.

"Our strategic plan, which is profoundly innovation-based, quality-oriented, and globally focused, will establish a network that will enable Webster University to function as a system, without any part having a preponderance in telling the other parts what to do," said Provost Julian Schuster. "The continuous interaction among all the parts will chart the movement of the entire system."

The plan's first theme, *Global Innovation through Inclusive Leadership*, seeks to strengthen Webster's leadership in global education. Achieving this goal starts with a curriculum in which a global feature will be included in every academic program. Such programs will be enhanced by strategic partnerships with local, regional, national, and international entities. Webster will continue to be a fertile ground for new initiatives and will maximize their effectiveness with the help of its distinct campus markets and populations. Finally, faculty, staff, and students will play an active role in leading the university into the future and will have opportunities to further develop their leadership skills.

The second theme, *A Global, Student-Centered Experience,* focuses on connecting students with each other, the faculty, and local and international campuses. Initiatives related to this theme include student collaborative research opportunities, the creation of an experiential learning center that serves students throughout the Webster network, and new programs in high-demand fields, including science, technology, engineering, mathematics, and medicine (STEMM).

A VISIONARY PLAN FOR THE FUTURE

In addition, Webster will develop student support systems across its network of campuses and support faculty and staff excellence in delivering student-centered experiences.

The third theme of the strategic plan is *A Network of Academic and Operational Excellence*. Such excellence is vital if Webster is "to be capable of competing with the best universities in every location where we have established a campus," Schuster said.

A broad range of initiatives are proposed toward this goal. First, the university will attract quality faculty through increasing endowed professorships and high-achieving students through specific recruitment efforts. In addition, it will enhance its services to graduates with graduate programs admissions and job placement assistance. Second, the university will offer opportunities to excel academically through an honors program, an enhanced Academic Resource Center, and "success coaches" for online students. Third, the university will investigate quick-response call centers and other ways to optimize communication throughout its network of

campuses. Fourth, the university will invest in comprehensive faculty-staff development through training.

Strategic and Sustainable Development is the fourth theme of the strategic plan. Quite simply, revenue growth will fund the first three themes of the plan and will ensure the overall health of Webster University.

That revenue growth will come from:

- increased enrollment among traditional undergraduate students, adult learners, graduate students, online students, and non-degree-seeking students in certification programs;

- endowments, alumni giving, and private contributions;

- efficient deployment and use of resources and environmental stewardship;

- strategic partnerships at local and global levels with the corporate, government, non-profit, and education sectors.

LUHR

EAST LOCKWOOD AVE

HOUSING / RETAIL

LIVING / LEARNING

LIVING / LEARNING

INTERDISCIPLINARY SCIENCES

STUDENT CENTER

LOBBY EXPANSION

GARDEN AVENUE

GARAGE

DINING

ARTS

BIG BEND BOULEVARD

ATHLETICS / RECREATION

HOUSING

EDGAR ROAD

A VISIONARY PLAN FOR THE FUTURE

Working together, the strategic plan's themes are designed to create "a distributed network of academic and operational excellence, and that excellence has to be everywhere, on every Webster University campus," Stroble said. St. Louis, Webster's historic home, will continue to have a "convening role" in the Webster University network and serve as a "gateway to the world," she added. "That doesn't mean the role is exclusive, however; the same can be true of any of our campuses." Added Schuster, "The administration of Webster University is in St. Louis, and that by itself sets the direction of the processes that currently exist. On the other hand, we do not want this to be a hierarchical organization, because a system is not efficient if it is highly hierarchical. An effective system needs to be based on distributive leadership in which all parts of the system will contribute to the mission, vision, and values of the institution."

Webster's network continues to grow to meet the needs of its students, faculty, and staff. In St. Louis, the progress to academic and operational excellence is evident in a master plan established in 2012 that defines a fifteen-to twenty-year effort. Central to the plan is the construction of an interdisciplinary sciences building for STEMM programs. Elsewhere in the system, Webster has moved its Vienna campus to a new, more visible location, opened a campus in Athens, and expanded to Ghana, Webster's first African campus.

The overall impact of all these efforts, together with the strategic plan, will be to create what Stroble calls "a global mindset that welcomes immersion in new ways of living and thinking."[59]

A global mindset will prepare Webster students for a changing and challenging future. "If you learn how to navigate a different country, a different language, a different culture, different politics and different lifestyles, that positions you to learn about new technologies, new field developments, and new environmental challenges in your lifetime," Stroble said. "It's about creating an open point of view about learning and changing and responding to an environment that will continue to change."[60]

Webster has developed a distinct advantage over other globally minded universities in

The Future

educating students for global citizenship. "What we have that few, if any, others have, is a commitment to operate as a system that has a robust global footprint," Schuster said. "Our continuous enhancement of our core operations solidifies our unique value proposition: When students come here, they will get a unique opportunity to study and to acquire competencies, skills, and knowledge to succeed in the global economy."[61]

Reflecting on Webster's past and its lessons for Webster's future, Stroble found that "it's intriguing to me to look at how our 100-year-history of resilience is a guidepost to our strategic planning and Centennial celebration."

She noted a pattern of challenges met by far-sighted leaders who turned those challenges to Webster's advantage. "That's what Webster has always done: questioned the status quo and created a new reality that was more compelling and more resonant with an increasingly globally diverse population," Stroble said. "That's what we've done. That's what we must continue to do."

"We know that, in the years ahead, there will be circumstances that will challenge us. What we hope to achieve is that the place and the concept we know as Webster University will indeed thrive in its next century and that we, just as those who came before us, will turn those circumstances to our advantage."

Global Impact for
THE NEXT CENTURY

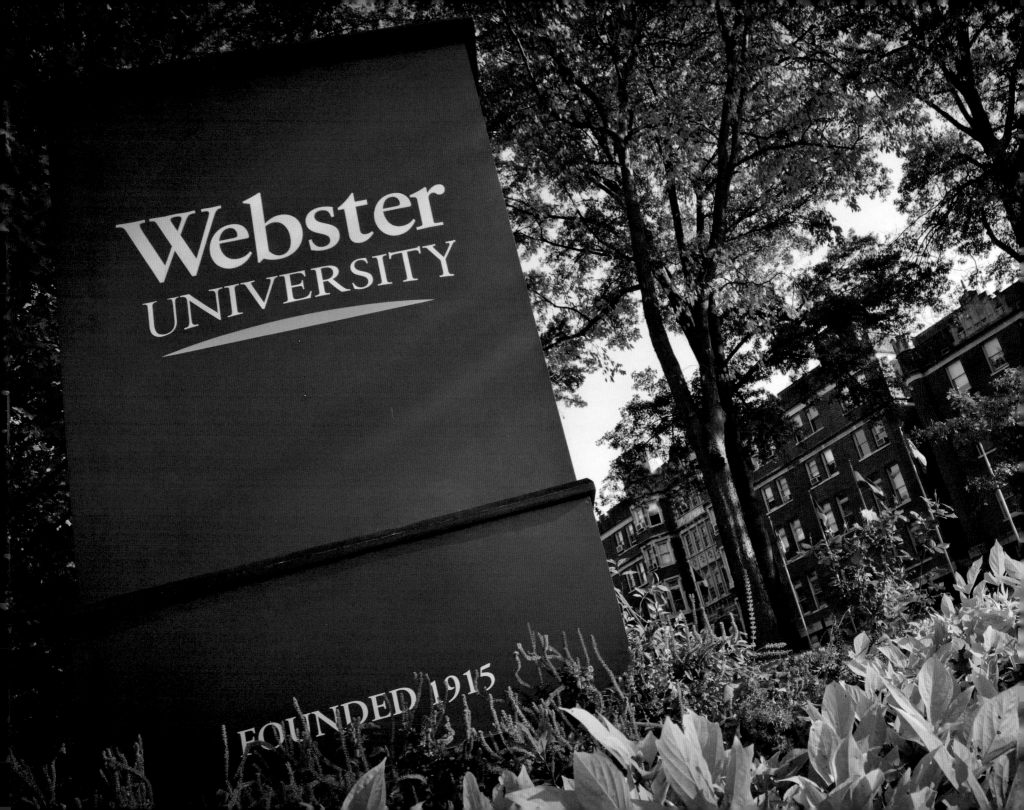

ENDNOTES

1. "The Law Enforcement Education Program Is in Serious Financial Disarray," Education, U.S. Government Accountability Office, 4 June 1980, http://www.gao.gov/products/FGMSD-80-46 (accessed 22 November 2014).

2. "Profiles of Community Leadership," Loretto Community, lorettocommunity.org, http://www.lorettocommunity.org/profiles-of-community-leadership/ (accessed 22 November 2014).

3. Jason Rosenbaum, "Residential infusion sparks transformation of downtown St. Louis' character," *St. Louis Beacon*, stlbeacon.org, https://www.stlbeacon.org/#!/content/31267/downtown_residential_development (accessed 23 November 2014).

4. Jacob Kirn, "Webster University to open downtown campus in Arcade Building," *St. Louis Business Journal*, bizjournals.com, http://www.bizjournals.com/stlouis/news/2014/06/03/webster-universityto-open-downtown-campus-in.html (accessed 23 November 2014).

5. "Loretto College Pageant," *St. Louis Post-Dispatch*, 2 June 1918, p. 7B. Ticket price found in "Students Preparing Pageant," *St. Louis Post-Dispatch*, 19 May 1918, p. 6B.

6. "Deaths by Country," By the Numbers, The National WWII Museum, nationalww2museum.org, http://www.nationalww2museum.org/learn/education/for-students/ww2-history/ww2-by-the-numbers/world-wide-deaths.html (accessed 30 November 2014).

7. "Vietnam War, Allied Troop Levels 1960-73," American War Library, americanwarlibrary.com, http://www.americanwarlibrary.com/vietnam/vwatl.htm (accessed 30 November 2014).

8. "Veterans Accelerated Urban Learning for Teaching, Program Development and Projection," Webster College, December 1968, http://files.eric.ed.gov/fulltext/ED027279.pdf (accessed 30 November 2014), p. 4

9. Ibid., 5-6, 17

10. "Sobering statistics for the Vietnam War," nationalvietnamveteransfoundation.org, http://www.nationalvietnamveteransfoundation.org/statistics.htm (accessed 1 December 2014).

11. "Webster University Vienna," http://www.ots.at presseaussendung/OTS_20110221_OTS0081/webster-university-vienna-30-jahre-und-kein-bisschen-leise (accessed 7 December 2014).

12. "Europe's largest cities," Citymayors Statistics, citymayors.com, http://www.citymayors.com/features/euro_cities1.html (accessed 15 December 2014).

13. "ACE Announces Ninth Internationalization Laboratory Cohort," Campus Internationalization, http://www.acenet.edu/news-room/Pages/Ninth-Internationalization-Laboratory-Cohort.aspx (accessed 14 December 2014).

14. Ibid.

15. George F. Donovan, "The Functions of a College Faculty," Report of the Proceedings and Addresses of the Thirty-Third Annual Meeting, New York, N.Y., April 14, 15, 16, 1936, *The National Catholic Educational Association Bulletin*, p. 258, http://www.mocavo.com/The-National-Catholic-Educational-Association-Bulletin-Report-of-the-Proceedings-and-Addresses-of-the-Thirty-Third-Annual-Meeting-New-York-N-Y-April-14-15-16-1936-Volume-Xxxiii/225323/265#262 (accessed 15 December 2014).

16. Jennifer Epstein, "In lieu of tenure." 10 March 2010, Inside Higher Education, https://www.insidehighered.com/news/2010/03/10/webster (accessed 5 March 2015).

17. "Best Film Series St. Louis 2014 – Webster Film Series," Arts and Entertainment, riverfronttimes.com, http://www.riverfronttimes.com/bestof/2014/award/best-film-series-2448764/ (accessed 16 December 2014).

18. "Webster University Film Series," short documentary video, https://www.youtube.com/watch?v=rvNje-CtZsg (accessed 16 December 2014).

19. PR Newswire, "Webster University Announces Inaugural '2012 Global Leaders in Residence' Program," Press Releases, *The Business Journals*, bizjournals.com, http://www.bizjournals.com/prnewswire/press_releases/2012/03/09/DC67936 (accessed 20 December 2014).

20. Sister Lucy Ruth Rawe, "Involved generation: Webster College." *Loretto Magazine*, vol. 12, no. 1, Fall 1970, pp. 4-5.

21. Edward Thomas Clark, "An evaluation of several aspects of the 'on-campus sabbatical' program at Webster College." (master's thesis, St. Louis University, 1970), 158-160.

22. "The New Breed of Teachers: Igniting the Individual Pupil," *Newsweek*, 26 September 1966, 106.

23. Ibid.

24. "Origins," University Without Walls, http://uwwhistory.org/origins/ (accessed 22 December 2014).

25. Susan C. Thomson, *St. Louis Post-Dispatch*, 5 March 2000, http://business.highbeam.com/435553/article-1G1-59963757/exteacher-record-donation-webster-u-fulfills-desire (accessed 22 February 2015).

26. Mark Bretz, *Ladue News*, 6 June 2013, laduenews.com, http://www.laduenews.com/diversions/arts-entertainment/q-a-with-marsha-mason/article_2158dbad-9e6c-5511-b585-9552b824f51d.html (accessed 15 March 2015).

27. "Elizabeth Wilde," SR/Olympic Sports, sports-reference.com, http://www.sports-reference.com/olympics/athletes/wi/elizabeth-wilde-1.html (accessed 27 December 2014).

28. "Key Dates In SLIAC History," St. Louis Intercollegiate Athletic Conference, sliac.org, http://www.sliac.org/information/Conf_Info/About/History (accessed 28 December 2014).

29. "Volleyball History & Records," St. Louis Intercollegiate Athletic Conference, sliac.org, http://www.sliac.org/sports/wvball/2014-15/files/Volleyball.pdf (accessed 28 December 2014).

30. "Conference Championship Summary," St. Louis Intercollegiate Athletic Conference, sliac.org, http://www.sliac.org/information/Championships/index (accessed 28 December 2014).

31. Jeff Starck, "Unlocking the Secrets of the Gorlok," *Webster-Kirkwood Times*, 14 September 2001, http://www.websterkirkwoodtimes.com/Articles-Webster-Groves-i-2001-09-14-178663.114137-Unlocking-The-Secrets-Of-The-Gorlock.html#axzz3N9jRwCXj (accessed 27 December 2014).

32. Ibid.

33. Ibid.

34. "All-Sports Award," St. Louis Intercollegiate Athletic Conference, sliac.org, http://www.sliac.org/information/Awards_Honors/All-Sports/index (accessed 28 December 2014).

35. "Webster University Baseball highlight video," Webster University Champions Award, St. Louis Sports Hall of Fame, http://www.stlouissportshalloffame.com/index.php?option=com_content&view=article&id=116&Itemid=383, 1:50.

36. "Early Productions," A History of The Repertory Theatre of St. Louis, repstl.org, http://www.repstl.org/history/P3/ (accessed 29 December 2014).

37. "A History of The Repertory Theatre of St. Louis," http://www.repstl.org/history/P0/ (accessed 29 December 2014).

38. "The Resident Company," A History of The Repertory Theatre of St. Louis, http://www.repstl.org/history/P2/ (accessed 29 December 2014).

39. "Webster University and Eden Theological Seminary Plan New Collaborations to Benefit Students and Faculty of Both Institutions," PR Newswire, http://www.prnewswire.com/news-releases/webster-university-and-eden-theological-seminary-plan-new-collaborations-to-benefit-students-and-faculty-of-both-institutions-78917027.html (accessed 30 December 2014).

40. Anne Midgette, "In 39th season, Opera Theatre of St. Louis shows good health, new work," 28 June 2014, *The Washington Post*, http://www.washingtonpost.com/entertainment/music/in-39th-season-opera-theatre-of-st-louis-shows-good-health-new-work/2014/06/26/7c43fdf8-fae1-11e3-8176-f2c941cf35f1_story.html (accessed 30 December 2014).

41. "SEEKING the nation's BEST musical theatre students," muny.org, http://www.muny.org/eya (accessed 1 January 2015).

42. Stacey Rynders, "Smart art: Everyone can study at universities' art collections and exhibits," 31 March 2006, *Sauce Magazine*, http://www.saucemagazine.com/a/11 (accessed 4 January 2015).

43. Ritter to Sister Matthew Marie, 28 March 1947, in Kemper, Donald J., "Catholic integration in St. Louis, 1935-1947," *Missouri Historical Review* 73, no. 1 (1978): 1-22.

44. Most of the material in this paragraph is taken from two sources: Philip Gleason, *Contending with Modernity: Catholic Higher Education in the Twentieth Century*, Oxford University Press, 1995, 237; and "The Heithaus Homily: February 11, 1944," Heithaus Haven, http://heithaush.blogspot.com/2013/02/heithaus-homily.html (accessed 5 January 2015).

45. Ellen Sherberg, "Leadership Styles," 9 September 2011, *St. Louis Business Journal*, bizjournals.com, http://www.bizjournals.com/stlouis/print-edition/2011/09/09/leadership-styles.html?page=2 (accessed 7 January 2015).

46. "Mission," About, Diversity Awareness Partnership, http://dapstl.org/about/ (accessed 8 January 2015).

47. Ibid.

48. Courtney Rubin, "Make the Leap to College and Land Well," 14 September 2012, *U.S. News and World Report*, http://www.usnews.com/education/best-colleges/articles/2012/09/14/make-the-leap-to-college-and-land-well (accessed 8 January 2015).

49. Mary Engel, "Blood-donor shortage in U.S. worsens," 6 September 2007, *Los Angeles Times*, seattletimes.com, http://seattletimes.com/html/health/2003870936_bloodshort06.html (accessed 10 January 2015).

50. Walbert Castillo, "Students travel to Ferguson for Spring Break to help rebuild the community", *USA Today*, usatoday,com, http://college.usatoday.com/2015/03/15/students-travel-to-ferguson-for-spring-break-to-help-rebuild-the-community/ (accessed 5 May 2015).

51. Alexander von Hoffman, "Why They Built the Pruitt-Igoe Project," http://www.soc.iastate.edu/sapp/PruittIgoe.html (accessed 10 January 2015).

52. Ibid.

53. Dana L. Spitzer, "Graduates of Upward Bound program return to aid others," *St. Louis Post-Dispatch*, June 29, 1967, 7W.

54. Correspondence from Margaret Frink to Blair Farrell, May 25, 1970.

55. Suzanne Reinhold, "Remembering Hiroshima and Nagasaki with WILPF," 28 July 2014, http://peaceeconomyproject.org/wordpress/?p=3273 (accessed 11 January 2015).

56. Lindsey Kingston, "The Rise of Human Rights Education: Opportunities, Challenges, and Future Possibilities," 25 August 2014, Societies Without Borders, https://societieswithoutborders.files.wordpress.com/2014/08/kingston.pdf (accessed 11 January 2015), 191.

57. Deborah Byrd, "Why celebrate Earth Day on April 22?" 22 April 2014, earthsky.org, http://earthsky.org/earth/this-date-in-science-why-celebrate-earth-day-on-april-22 (accessed 14 January 2015).

58. Gregory Jones, "Elizabeth Stroble and Webster University are helping to turn St. Louis into a Gateway to the World," Smart Business, 1 May 2013, sbnonline.com, http://www.sbnonline.com/article/elizabeth-stroble-and-webster-university-are-helping-to-turn-st-louis-into-a-gateway-to-the-world/ (accessed 2 April 2015).

59. Rahul Chouduha, "Success with global engagement strategies requires a systemic integration of diverse university elements interview," DrEducation: International Higher Education Blog, Feb. 2015, Dr.Education.com, http://www.dreducation.com/2015/02/webster-university-president-global.html (accessed 11 March 2015).

60. Jones.

61. Ibid.

PHOTO AND PUBLIC ART CREDITS

Photo Credits

p. 58, "Easy to Spot" by Mariah Nadler (bottom middle)

p. 60, "Venice Traffic" by Amy Alderson

p. 61, "The Girl on the Stairs" by Shannon Bucklin (left); "Eufrazijeva Bazilika" by Yvonne Osei (top right)

p. 145, *The Journal* Newsroom by Natalia Martinez

p. 219, Photos (top) by Jerry Naunheim Jr.

p. 222-223, Photos by Ken Howard

p. 224, Photo by Phillip Hamer

p. 251, "Ferguson Rally" by Matt Duchesne

Public Art Credits

p. 237,

Cavallo e Cavaliere by Marino Marini (top left)

Swingers by Robert Zakanitch (bottom left)

Window 1/3 by Jene Highstein (middle)

Horn by Gary Passanise (right)